HUGHESIE!

HUGHESIE!

An autobiography by

Mark Hughes

with David Meek

The Red Dragon

MAINSTREAM
PUBLISHING

EDINBURGH AND LONDON

First published in Great Britain in 1994 by
MAINSTREAM PUBLISHING COMPANY (EDINBURGH) LTD
7 Albany Street
Edinburgh EH1 3UG

ISBN 1 85158 680 6

A catalogue record for this book is available from the British Library

Typeset in Bembo by Servis Filmsetting Ltd, Manchester
Printed in Great Britain by Butler and Tanner Ltd, Frome

CONTENTS

FOREWORD

by Alex Ferguson
Manager, Manchester United

MARK HUGHES is a warrior with whom you could trust your life. He has just completed the best ever season of his career, maintaining an unbelievably high standard and never wavering as a fierce competitor.

He has had ten great years at Old Trafford after arriving here from school in Wrexham and, though he went away for a couple of years to sample European football with Barcelona and Bayern Munich, I think he was glad to return. I certainly made it a priority when I was appointed manager of Manchester United to try to buy him back. I remember telling the chairman at the time that here was a player who fully intended to play every game and make a positive contribution in each one.

It's a quality I look for when I am assessing a player to work at Old Trafford and Mark has it in abundance. You search for enthusiasm and I have never regretted my decision to make him a United player again. Some people say you should never go back in life, and I know what they mean, but this particular return has worked brilliantly for both the club and player.

I was glad to see him enjoy a successful testimonial after our Championship success last May. The question of testimonials for well-paid players is a controversial issue for many people these days but they are a fact of life and a key factor in determining the movement of top-class players. In Mark's case, he could easily have decided to stay in Spain or Germany but with the prospect of a testimonial match after ten years with us we were able to persuade him to return to Old Trafford. The transfer has worked out well for him but at the same time, I don't think anyone could suggest that he has not given more than a fair return to Manchester United.

Since Eric Cantona's arrival he has shared in a partnership which, in years to come, people may well deem was made in heaven. Both players have significant egos which could have resulted in a clash but which, in fact, have gelled. They have proved the perfect foil for one another's talents and their personalities have brought the best out of each other. They share this great desire to entertain and Mark has seen the arrival of Eric as the ultimate challenge. He has become an outstanding team player as well as a scorer of great goals, as was emphasised last season, which I think was the best he has ever had for Manchester United. Mark has always had a great aura but now he is contributing much more. The pair of them have created a very potent partnership which, last season, produced 47 goals between them, the best figures from a pair of strikers at United for many years. Their goals have certainly been a telling factor in our trophy collection of the last two years.

Mark has become an idol for many fans. They like his commitment and see in him a present-day Denis Law, especially as a scorer of spectacular goals. Personally, I like the way he puts injuries out of his mind. He barely misses a fixture, giving the impression of being armour-plated. His willingness to compete up the middle on his own when necessary and his refusal to shrink from the most punishing markers is like waving a flag of courage for the rest of the team. All his team-mates know that when they play the ball forward for him to hold while they get up the field, he is not going to lose it in a hurry.

You take a lot of hard knocks playing at the sharp end, as I know to my cost as a one-time striker, and so I have always watched with particular interest to see how the front men react to punishment. I have no hesitation in saying that Sparky is the most courageous striker in the game. Centre-backs know before they even go out that no matter how much they try to kick him off the park he will come back for more. No matter how much punishment he takes, it is all like water off a duck's back to Mark. His amazing durability gives him a tremendous advantage. Others would fold under the kind of hostility he comes up against but he totally frustrates his markers by getting up, dusting himself down and carrying on with the job. I cannot speak too highly of his resilience.

Away from football, Mark does not fit the public's perception of him. The flamboyant star is really a very quiet, shy guy who prefers to head away from the bright lights to be with his family and perhaps go back to his roots in Wales. The terror of defences turns into a mild-mannered gent once he leaves the environs of football.

The only time you see him angry is when he is not in the first team. If I leave him out he is like a bear with a sore head for about three weeks. He is, in fact, murder to have around the place. He regards the axe as an insult. His pride is hurt and he is genuinely upset. I always explain patiently my reasons when I occasionally leave him out but they just go over his head. He doesn't want explanations, just his number 10 shirt, and at the end of the day that's an ambition which cannot be faulted.

Manager, players and fans alike are particularly indebted to Mark for one golden moment last season as we chased our Premiership and FA Cup double. We reached a moment of crisis in extra time of our Cup semi-final tie against Oldham at Wembley. Oldham were ahead with just 50 seconds of extra time remaining and there was probably more than just the Cup at stake when Mark leaned back to score a great equaliser. He saved the match for us. We went on to win the replay and picked up our rhythm again in the League to clinch the Championship. If we had been knocked out of the Cup, not only would the Double have disappeared, but we might not even have won the League in the face of such disappointment.

Mark Hughes saves his goals for the right time. His specialty has always been to score the vital ones at important moments, none more so than his super strike last May. He's a man who mostly keeps his opinions to himself, so I am looking forward to reading his book, which like his performances will, I am sure, be penetrating and meaningful.

Alex Ferguson

PREFACE

MANCHESTER UNITED are the best and we have got the medals to prove it: back to back Championships capped by an elusive League and FA Cup double. What a thrilling and challenging time we have had at Old Trafford these past couple of seasons. I am so proud to have been a part of this fabulous era, which will obviously go down as one of the golden periods in the distinguished history of the club.

It hasn't been glory all the way since I joined as a shy boy straight from school in Wrexham some 15 years ago, and, of course, I had two traumatic years abroad with Barcelona and Bayern Munich before Alex Ferguson brought me back home to share in his great United adventure.

There is no doubt, though, that the theatre of dreams has staged a smash-hit lately and this would seem an appropriate time for me to set down the story of my life and times with Manchester United.

Who knows what the future will bring? The only real certainty about football is its uncertainty and the game never stands still. I know Manchester United is where my heart lies as well as my professional career, and if it is left to me I will play for the Reds until it is time to hang up my boots. The place is so special, especially the supporters, who have a passion and enthusiasm which spills on to the field and who gave me a marvellous testimonial match last season to mark my ten years as a senior player.

Along with my wife, Jill, and my family, I would like to dedicate my book to the supporters who have breathed the fire into this proud Red Dragon.

Chapter One

STILL HUNGRY

I HAVE, in fact, won much more than medals lately. Just as important for me has been the satisfaction of laying to rest a criticism that was beginning to haunt me. The idea went round at one stage of my career that Mark Hughes was difficult to play with, and following my return from Spain and Germany there were people suggesting that Manchester United would have to get rid of me because it had become impossible to find a man I could hit it off with up front.

So thank you very much indeed, Eric Cantona, a player who, in my view, has given United in general a new dimension and me in particular a first-class partner. We may not speak the same language, but I think I can safely say that from time to time we make the ball talk louder than words. It's not really for me to say how well I am playing these days, but I think, without being unduly immodest, that I have played my part in our run of success. I certainly feel as if I have made a reasonable contribution, and I know that the Frenchman has changed my footballing life.

There was a touch of luck about his transfer to Old Trafford from Leeds in November 1992. It was an open secret that Alex Ferguson wanted David Hirst from Sheffield Wednesday and the club even announced at their annual meeting of shareholders that they had made yet another approach to the Hillsborough club. In the end the manager bought Dion Dublin from Cambridge – only to find the lanky striker smashing his ankle in his fourth first-team game of season 1992–93. Then a few weeks later it seemed almost an afterthought, when, following an inquiry from Leeds about Denis Irwin, the club asked about the availability of the Frenchman.

I think the boss was as surprised as anyone when Leeds said yes, he could leave Elland Road. What we didn't know at the time, of course, was that Eric had been having problems with Howard Wilkinson and the Leeds manager had come to the conclusion that a parting of the ways would be in the best interests of both club and player. It was certainly a lucky break for Manchester United, though at first the papers were in overdrive highlighting the Frenchman's disciplinary record, and let's face it, Eric has had his moments. I must admit that at first I wondered whether it would end in tears with us as well, but it didn't take me long to take a different view.

In fact, he had only been on the pitch a few moments when I said to myself *this guy will do for me!* Eric's first appearance for us came in December 1992 when he took over from Ryan Giggs at half-time against Manchester City at Old Trafford. He had started on the substitutes' bench because we had just won two games, including a valuable 1-0 victory at Arsenal. It's always difficult hitting the pace when you come on as a sub, especially in a derby, and I suppose overall Eric didn't do a lot. But there was one moment early in the second half when he suddenly got clear down the right to knock in a great cross. I wasn't expecting it and I am afraid I made a mess of my attempt to score with a header. At the same time

I thought the fellow can certainly play a bit, and if he carries on like that I'll score more than I miss.

His ability is obvious. He is a big man but he has a touch which at times can be as light as a feather. It's his first touch which is so impressive, whether it is to kill the ball, play it first time, or hit quality passes with the inside of his foot. I must say, he has brought something special to the whole team, and I am not embarrassed to admit that we all try to copy him. He has opened new doors for us and he showed us that we needed to be more ambitious in our personal play. Now, thanks mainly to Eric's example, we actually try to outdo him, so much so that at one stage I think we worried Alex Ferguson. In one team talk he said, 'All these flicks and things, leave them to Eric because he can do them and you can't.' We all burst out laughing, but he had a point. Anyway, he has taught us a lot, not least making us more aware of the European way of playing.

What I mean is that Eric will give a short pass, expecting you to give it straight back to him; conversely, he is always ready to accept a short ball and return it almost in the same movement. Most English players would consider that a complete waste of time, and possibly a lot of supporters would find it negative and boring, but they miss the point. What Eric is trying to do is change the pattern of opponents around him, because though he might not have moved, the opposition probably have done, and so a gap might have opened up that he can exploit. It's a more Continental style, but I believe it adds something to our game and nowadays you might well see United players exchanging this kind of pass not involving Eric at all.

You all know what I am talking about because you have seen him in action, but I must also tell you that he can be even more remarkable in training when he tries still more outrageous tricks. Professional footballers are not easily impressed, because they see good footballers all the time, but

I tell you, our Frenchman has opened our eyes a good many times. Very often we simply stop playing and clap in admiration. It's amazing what he can do with the ball, especially when he ties someone up in knots with one of his little juggling stunts.

He doesn't do it to embarrass anyone, he just loves showing off his footballing skills. All you can do is hope and pray you are not one of his victims and therefore the target of the laughs which will come your way. It's all good-natured stuff really because we know how much we owe the big man. His arrival somehow flicked a switch on in the team which took us from being a good side to one that started to win things on a regular basis.

His example rubbed off on the rest of us. Call us Cantona copycats if you like, but he has given us the confidence to try things that before we would have been too embarrassed and frightened of attempting. I don't see it as a coincidence that since his arrival we have become champions twice and Double winners!

Eric still doesn't speak much English. I think he gets the gist of what's going on around him but, like me when I was in Spain, because I couldn't express myself I ended up saying little. It will never be easy for him to share in typical dressing-room banter but you can sense that he tries hard to fit in and the fact that he is trying shows that he wants to be part of the club. I don't think he has tried as hard at some of the other clubs he has been with. I believe he is in the right place for his talents and temperament now. I think he has settled and, though we all realise that one day he will move on, I don't think it will be for some time yet. He has got the taste for Manchester United and that's good news for the rest of us. Something very dramatic will have to blow up in his face for him to walk away from Old Trafford. We as players have a part to play in keeping him at United. We must encourage his involvement to make sure he is happy. He still lives over at Leeds, where his wife is settled in a job at the university teaching French, but he doesn't let the motorway cut him off too much. He has joined us socially on a few occasions. We have all met his wife and he sometimes brings his son to the training ground, where he plays with Peter Schmeichel's boy, which might have broadened his horizons a bit because Casper is a bundle of mischief. I know from my experience during my testimonial that if Eric says he will do something, he does it. He supported several of my sportsmen's evenings, golf days and charity events and never let me down. He even bought one of my testimonial ties!

The manager had to stretch a few principles to accommodate a Frenchman who is his own man and who obviously has had his problems conforming with certain requirements. Alex Ferguson didn't exactly rewrite the rule book but he treated him differently and explained to the rest of us that Eric was a special player requiring special treatment. On the field, if I had tried some of the outrageous fancy flicks you see Eric performing, I would probably have got a right rollicking but our maestro gets away with it, and rightly so. Off the field, the manager is more ready to laugh than get annoyed if Eric turns up wearing some of his way-out gear for a formal occasion which would find the rest of us in big trouble. We were all in blazers, collars and ties at Manchester Town Hall to meet the Lord Mayor when Eric arrived looking as if he was on his way to a disco. The manager smiled, and because Eric is in a different class as a player and personality we all go along with the idea of him being a special case.

At the same time, I think we have given Eric the kind of football, mystique and success that he craves. I know he enjoys the way we play. Leeds were taking the long-ball route when he was at Elland Road and I don't think he thought much of it. Certainly, he was out of step with Howard Wilkinson, which, of course, is how we came to get him. As I say, it was Leeds United's loss and our gain, especially mine because since he arrived I have enjoyed probably my best ever season. The myth that I am a problem player in terms of finding a suitable partner in attack has been well and truly dispelled.

My problems in this department started after I had come back to England to rejoin United in 1988. It looked a dream ticket: Brian McClair and myself as the new pairing up front. I certainly expected it to take off and produce a stack of goals. After all, the previous season had seen Choccy become the first player to score more than 20 League goals in a season since United's glory years in the Sixties. Most people considered that I would help rather than hinder Brian to get even more goals, while at the same time hitting the target myself in a big way.

Alas, it didn't work out. Brian had certainly done extremely well the season before I arrived. I think he got 24 League goals in a total of around 30 or more, which was good by any standards and certainly something new for United. Unfortunately, the system changed to accommodate yours truly. Once I had arrived, Brian played either in midfield or as a deep player coming into the box on late runs and, later, even on the flanks. We were never played together as a pair of orthodox strikers, definitely not in the way Eric and I have been playing. Neither Brian nor I had the return of goals in our first season together, 1988–89, that was expected of us. People came to the conclusion that we couldn't play together and that I was too much of an individual to team up successfully with a partner. From that, it followed that no one could play with me.

But there were other factors as well. For instance, within a month or so of me joining the club, United suddenly had no wingers. Gordon Strachan and Jesper Olsen left the club and Peter Davenport, who I'm told had done extremely well for Brian McClair, also moved on. The supply line for the strikers had gone and Brian and I carried the can. I don't think it was so much a personal failure as a shift in the tactical emphasis. I was particularly criticised for hanging on to the ball too long. From my point of view, the problem was that I had no one to pass it to. Because there were no wingers, the midfield players were reluctant to make early runs and I always felt that if I gave a bad ball through trying to use it early I was only putting our defence under pressure.

The whole situation has changed now. For one thing, we have been playing with wingers again. Indeed, we have three top-class players in Ryan Giggs, Lee Sharpe and Andrei Kanchelskis competing for two places. Then, in addition, there is Eric. Some people see him as an old-fashioned inside-forward, creating and scoring goals. Whatever, he's certainly a dream to play with.

My first partner as a striker at Old Trafford was Norman Whiteside. We played together in the junior teams, the youth side and then the reserves. He was 18 months younger than me but he was such a big, strong lad – they always said he was a man at the age of 14 – that he got into the first team before me. It wasn't until he was converted into a midfield player that I began to get into the League team. My partner then was Frank Stapleton and I think we did OK. He was a creative striker and we played well together. In my first full season I got around 26 goals in all competitions while Frank got his normal quota of about 16. It was rated a successful partner-ship and there was no comment in those days that I was diffi-cult to play with.

Unfortunately, Frank was coming towards the end of his career and we had only one more season together before I left United to spread my wings with Barcelona. That final season was another good one for me, though. I notched 17 goals in the League, most of them in the first half of the season and I must have been doing something right to attract the attention of the Spanish club.

Looking back, I think United missed an opportunity when they failed to play Norman and me together as strikers in the first team. I can understand Ron Atkinson's reluctance in a way because we were both young and inexperienced but we had done well enough at a lower level and I would have fancied having a go with Norman up front. He was always an aggressive player and I'm fairly determined in my approach as well. Together, I think we might have shaken a few people up because in addition to our strength I think we both enjoyed a fair amount of skill. I certainly always had the highest regard for his technique and ability. In my view, he was the best player at the club at that time. People go on about his aggression but at the end of training on a Friday we always spent an hour or so shooting at goal and Norman easily had the best finishing rate. He would tuck 80 per cent of his shots away. The goalkeepers, such as Gary Bailey, Steve Pears and Jeff Wealands, knew where the ball was going but couldn't do anything about it.

Anyway, we were never given the chance and my next partner after Frank Stapleton was Gary Lineker at the Nou Camp in Spain. Gary was at his peak. He had scored something like 40 goals for Everton the season before and he had been the top scorer at the World Cup for England that summer. Incidentally, Gary was bought to play with me and not the other way round, though I have to admit that he gave Barcelona a better return on their investment than they ever got with me. I suppose it has to be said that this was another partnership that simply did not work out. I was relatively young and inexperienced; Gary was very single-minded about goal-scoring. At that stage of my career, I didn't attach as much significance to my goal tally. I was satisfied if I had played well overall. Indeed, I thought it better to turn in a good performance, regardless of whether I finished with any goals.

Gary realised that all Barcelona really wanted from a striker was goals. He had more experience than me and he was perhaps more streetwise. He shrewdly identified the priority and in his first year he finished as the second highest scorer in Europe after Hugo Sanchez, who invariably topped the list. Gary profited from our partnership and I didn't. It led to an unhappy time for me. I was farmed out to Bayern Munich with Steve Archibald taking over my role until the end of the season. Then, Barcelona kissed and made up with Berndt Schuster, who had fallen out seriously with the club, and really that was the end of my Spanish holiday.

My other great partner in football has been Ian Rush with Wales, in many ways similar to Gary Lineker, especially if we are talking about scoring rates. In my view, Rushie works harder for the team, though. Gary is not going to tackle back for you. Certainly, he will score important goals in big games. Ian will do that as well, as his magnificent record with Liverpool shows, but he does more than that – and playing for Wales, he has to! We've always had quality up front in the Welsh team but mostly we have had a problem getting the ball up to the forwards – not an easy job, of course, as I discovered for myself when I was shifted to a midfield role.

Most Welsh teams have to battle to keep the other team out, with the emphasis on destruction rather than construction. When I was up front I always enjoyed the partnership, and I might just point out that when we first got together we went 16 or 17 games without a defeat. Critics who want to be negative about Wales forget that. Ian was always an important cog in the Liverpool machine that dominated English football for two decades. It made him a winner, and a winner in style. He brings the same quality to his international football and demands it from the whole squad. He can get quite frustrated at times because he expects such a lot but his commitment to Welsh football cannot be questioned.

He's a very fair player, what I would call a players' player, and when you speak to fellow professionals about him, you discover that they all hold him in the greatest respect – not just as a player but as a person, too. People who have attained only a tenth of what Ian has achieved can get a bit above themselves but that's never been a problem for him and players appreciate that.

Mike Smith, who has just taken over again as manager of Wales, tells me he is thinking of playing me up front once more at international level, and if that is how it works out I know I will enjoy playing alongside Rushie again. More vital for my long-term future, though, is the matter of playing for Manchester United and the possibility of the club signing another top-class striker.

Alex Ferguson has already made one move in that direction by snapping up Graeme Tomlinson from Bradford, a young forward of great potential, I'm told. Then during the summer the boss indicated he was interested in Chris Sutton, until Norwich demanded a £5m fee and our club had second thoughts! Now Sutton is at Blackburn with Alan Shearer and clearly it threatens to be an outstanding combination. That's what they said when I came home from Spain to play alongside Choccy. You can never be sure. Will they be as good together as Eric and me? We will see. Maybe the boss will look elsewhere for an English striker to offset the fact that Eric and I are both deemed foreign for the purposes of the European Cup. Certainly, he likes to keep a competitive edge in every department, and he moved swiftly during the summer when David May ran out of contract at Blackburn.

I know to my cost how good a defender he is because he hardly gave me a kick when we played at Ewood Park late in the season and lost 2-0. I got so frustrated I lost my temper for a fraction of a second and was rightly booked. David will do well for us if he maintains that standard. He is not particularly big but he wins a fair amount in the air, he's wiry and gets stuck in. He is also a good reader of the game, and of course he is English, which fits the bill as the manager strengthens the squad to cope with the UEFA rule which limits you to five non-English players in your squad for European competitions.

The additional problem for us up front is that Eric has gone into this season with a four-match ban in Europe, which will wipe him out of most of the opening group ties. Everyone at United is desperate to do well in the European Cup after flopping abroad for the last two seasons, which is why I think the club first had Sutton, an Englishman, in their sights. But even without his arrival there is still an intense degree of competition for places. The boys at the back now have to look at David May, and even without Sutton it's the same for us up front. Brian McClair has been under pressure ever since Eric Cantona was signed and I would imagine Dion Dublin is jumping up and down with impatience as he waits for a run rather than occasional appearances. The battle royal among the wingers won't be any easier either, while more and more of our young stars are going to step up the challenge.

So what does the future hold for Mark Hughes?

The competition and challenge don't frighten me. If the manager wasn't building for the future he wouldn't be doing his job. I have seen a few off in the past and I consider I am still good enough to hold my own. With the help of a rejuvenated side playing with good wingers and with Eric in the team, I have just turned in probably my best ever season, so why should I be afraid? I believe I have three or four more years left at the top and I hope they will all be spent at United. I have one more year left on my contract and by the time you read this book I hope to have signed another one to keep me playing in a red shirt. You don't want to leave a club like this because once you do you are going downhill. It is all happening at Old Trafford these days and I want to be part of it for a bit longer.

I'm philosophical about the situation. If I am playing well I will expect to be in the side, and the way I have been playing, with a revived scoring tally, I have the confidence to think I will be in the side. If not, I am always mindful of the fact that when I got my chance as a youngster it was at the expense of some other established star. However, don't confuse a philosophical attitude with a slackening in the old Red Dragon's ambition and commitment to football.

I know I had a tremendous testimonial last May, and it rewarded me handsomely from the financial point of view, but I have no intention of sneaking off into a quiet corner somewhere to count my money. Maybe there are players who reach testimonial stage and begin to let themselves go a bit because they can't see what else there is to play for. So let me tell you that there is still a fire burning in the Hughes belly with a real desire to keep playing football and win things with Manchester United. At the start of each season the manager always asks one particular question. He demands to know if we are still hungry for success, because, as he goes on to explain, if the players lose their ambition and appetite to win things then all of us will all be wasting our time. I know I shall be able to look him in the eye and assure him I am ready for more!

I think we have proved we have the right attitude by overcoming the two crises which have faced us in the last three years. First of all, we had to cope with the bitter disappointment of appearing to have the Championship in the bag in 1992 only to falter on the last lap and see Leeds race past for the title. There was a real danger that we would be overtaken by despair and the feeling that Manchester United were simply not meant to become champions. I guess we proved the doubters wrong about that by hitting back the very next season, 1992–93, to go all the way and end the 26-year wait for the Championship at Old Trafford.

Then, of course, we were confronted by the reverse challenge. Would we sit back and rest on our laurels with the feeling that the job was done? Well, I think we made clear our attitude on that one by retaining our Championship crown and reaching the two domestic Cup finals as we chalked up our 1994 League and FA Cup double. So I can't see any softening in our resolve this season, and you can be sure that Alex Ferguson will not tolerate any slackness that might creep in.

As I see it, there is only one way to play football and that's to win. Old Trafford is a fantastic place, but only when you are winning. It can be quite hostile and murderous if things go wrong for any length of time because expectations are high. Quite rightly, the fans who make us the best-supported club in the country, with all that that means financially, expect a good return. If they don't get it, then watch out and run for cover, and believe me, when the United fans are right behind you there is no better feeling, but if they start to groan it's a killer. I don't blame them. I am sure I would do the same if I was in the stands and felt I wasn't getting a fair return for my money and support.

We can't expect to win everything for ever, but having clawed our way to the top the next battle is to make sure we stay there, challenging for everything and aiming to maintain the consistency which has been the feature of our game in recent seasons.

Personally, I consider it easier to stay successful once you have established yourself in that class. Confidence is such a big element in winning, and at the same time I think the pressure eases. The weight of expectation during our first Championship season was really unbelievable; but with that first one in the bag we simply went out with a song in our hearts to win it again. The manager keeps insisting that we should go out and enjoy ourselves, and I think he is right. Let's face it, these are the good times and we should make the most of them. They are a darned sight better than the bad times, and I know what I am talking about because I have had a few lows in my career.

Overall, I have been very fortunate, with more ups than downs – and, in a business which provides relatively few winners, that is saying a great deal. Obviously, we must keeping striving, and if any of us ever needs inspiration they need only consider Bryan Robson, who left us in the summer for player-management with Middlesbrough.

Right up to the very last match of the season, in which he played, he was burning with desire to hold down a regular place in the first team. The fact that he was 37 made no difference to his commitment or determination to be a winner. Paul Ince and Roy Keane had robbed him of his permanent position, and the place was bursting with thrusting young midfield players, but it made no difference to Bryan, who worked just as hard as he had done as a young man. He invariably led the pack in training, always busting a gut to finish first in the running routines, and then when he did play always setting his usual high standard, driving and inspiring those around him.

He was always a naturally fit man and a good athlete, but towards the end of his career what did he really have to prove? He had been there, seen that, done this, won that; he had done everything, in fact, but he never lost his desire to play and win. Robbo was an example to us all and I am glad he played long enough to share in our success of recent seasons. It would have been a shame if he had gone out of the game without a Championship medal, for instance.

Anyway, he has gone off now to try his hand at management and I wish him luck. Of course, there are a few other faces missing this season, with the manager deciding to trim his squad to make way for new signings and the youth revolution that has been quietly taking place at Old Trafford. The boys who won the FA Youth Cup a couple of years ago are now young men and they are starting to knock on the door of the senior squad.

They are a talented bunch, with players such as wingers Keith Gillespie, capped for Northern Ireland this season, and Ben Thornley, whose rich promise has only been delayed by a serious knee injury. Then there are midfielders Nicky Butt, David Beckham and Paul Scholes, along with defenders such as Gary Neville and Chris Casper.

I expect we shall see a little more of them this season after saying goodbye to the likes of Clayton Blackmore, Mike Phelan, Lee Martin, Darren Ferguson, Danny Wallace and Les Sealey. A lot of the characters have gone with that little lot, and I shall particularly miss my Welsh team-mate, Clayton. We came through the junior teams together, as well as playing many times for Wales, and injuries gave him a raw deal in his last year. I hope he has better luck playing for Robbo at Middlesbrough. I am sure he will prove a big hit at Ayresome Park.

The dressing-rooms at Old Trafford and the training ground won't quite seem the same. The young lads who take their places in the squad will be quieter, but they will remind those of us still lucky enough to be at Old Trafford that we must deliver the goods or make way for someone else who can.

Chapter Two

LOADSA BOTTLE

SO who has no bottle now?

It seems Manchester United just have to lose a couple of games and immediately the critics come rushing in to say we are losing our nerve and haven't got the mental strength to go all the way to the finishing line.

I suppose people first got the idea into their heads that we were brittle when we faltered in the closing stages of the race with Leeds three years ago and they were looking for reasons for our so-called collapse. There may have been an element of truth in the accusation that year because the weight of expectation after 25 years, as it was then, without the League title did indeed put tremendous pressure on the players.

However, we learned from that bitter experience and roared back the following season finally to nail the elusive League title. Then for good measure last season we resisted a tremendous challenge from Blackburn to pull off the difficult feat of staying champions for two successive seasons with a couple of Cup finals thrown in to underline the fact that it was no fluke. We are only the fourth club since the war to win the Championship in successive seasons. Portsmouth went back-to-back immediately after the war and the Busby Babes managed it before the Munich disaster, followed by Wolves. Liverpool in their golden era did it three times, including a treble, and now we have joined this select group. It's not easy, as the record books tell you.

So I think I can safely say that the charge of lacking bottle is another criticism that has been well and truly booted into touch. I was certainly surprised when a few of the more lurid tabloid papers started to suggest we were losing control of ourselves in the closing stages of last season.

It came to a head when we went to play at Blackburn in early April after a storming run by the Rovers had brought them on to our shoulders, while we had lost at home to Chelsea and squandered a few more points with two or three disappointing draws, including one against bottom club Swindon.

Gary Pallister did a radio interview on Club Call which was picked up by a few of the papers who claimed he had suggested that Blackburn wouldn't have the nerve to go all the way. What, in fact, he was saying was that as the pressure built up we possibly had the advantage of having been down that road twice before – once coming a cropper but the next time producing the necessary resolve to finish successfully as winners. Gary argued that Blackburn, facing the pressure for the first time with their present team, might find it as hard as we had done, which I think was a fair point.

By the time the headline writers had finished, though, it looked as if Pally was accusing Blackburn of a lack of bottle, and quite naturally Alan Shearer hit back after their 2-0 win against us at Ewood Park. Who has the bottle now? he wanted to know.

Well, I suppose we had the final word and I hope no one

will taunt us on the issue again. Actually, I don't think winning and losing at football comes down to courage in that way. The determination and commitment of a team rarely wavers, and in my opinion results are mainly decided by a whole range of factors, including form, confidence, lucky refereeing decisions and the quality of the players involved.

I know our manager wasn't impressed by the war of words with Blackburn because he promptly put a ban on interviews and said that until the Championship was either won or lost we mustn't talk to the media. There had been two or three other incidents which had hit the headlines in a big way, notably the sending-off of Peter Schmeichel and then the dismissal of Eric Cantona in successive League games. I think the manager had also found himself being carried away a little when he exploded and called Jimmy Hill a prat.

Anyway, after the Blackburn game he decided to cool it with the media and he told us that we were paid to play football rather than talk about it. This led to suggestions that we were adopting a siege mentality and that we were becoming paranoid, but I don't think people always realise the demands of public relations at a high-profile club like Manchester United. For instance, we have much-increased calls these days from our own club enterprises, which now include a monthly magazine as well as the match programme. Last season, the club also introduced its own radio station, which broadcasts interviews as well as match commentaries. Then there are demands from our superstore to model Manchester United gear, sponsors to be met and various functions to attend, as well as charity calls.

Don't get me wrong. I am not complaining, because the modern professional footballer accepts that he is required to play his part in the commercial operation which helps fund the whole expensive organisation. But there is a danger of losing sight of the main purpose, and talking a good game doesn't win matches. So I think Alex Ferguson was very shrewd when he stepped in to focus our minds on the essentials.

As soon as the title was in the bag we returned to normal and by the time we were preparing for the final of the FA Cup we had an open day for the media. I might add that we didn't have what is referred to as a 'players' pool', whereby television, radio and the papers are required to make a donation for an interview or photograph. The manager argued that we are paid enough these days without bringing in an agent to take advantage of a big occasion like a Wembley final and squeeze a few bob out of the press.

So the boss is not all bad for the press, and indeed he devotes a lot of time to projecting the image of the club and maintaining a rapport with the fans via the media channels. The last few weeks of the season were very tense, though, and so he made a decision which subsequent events showed to be correct. After all, you cannot argue with a season which for the first time ever saw a club win the League and reach *both* domestic Cup finals.

In fact, we knocked club records down like ninepins. Our tally of 92 points was the highest since the introduction of three points for a win, and it matched the record of Sir Matt Busby's team of 1957, which, translated into present-day points figures, also took the title with 92. We lost only four League games, and the last time a United team did better than that was way back in 1906 in a season of only 38 games in the Second Division. We are the only team, other than Liverpool in their heyday, to win five major trophies in five years, and so it goes on. What was particularly pleasing was that we were not only able to match the Babes' successive Championships but we went on to notch United's first League and FA Cup double and so become only the fourth side this century to complete the historic twosome.

Statistics tell only half the story, though, and cannot express the emotion and satisfaction that swept round Old

Trafford on the night we played Southampton after becoming champions following Blackburn's failure at Coventry. Over and over again the cry went round Old Trafford: '*Championes*', the chant that is a mixture of Miles Platting and Milan, made popular by televised Italian football. It was a tremendous experience and the tributes flowed in. I was particularly appreciative of the words of Terry Venables, the England manager and my boss when I was with Barcelona, who said: 'People not involved will be pleased that they have won it because of the way they play the game. There is a cockiness about their play. They are extrovert in many ways. They put such skill together. It is beginning to look as if they can have the kind of era enjoyed by Liverpool when they dominated for so long and won the Championship 11 times in the Seventies and Eighties.'

I am certainly proud of my own contribution and the goals which came from the strike-force of Eric Cantona and me. Between us in all competitions we notched 47, with 25 to Eric and 22 for myself, my best since I got a similar figure in my first full season in the senior side ten years ago. And, as Alex Ferguson says, if you have your two front men scoring over 40 goals between them then you are in business for honours.

So how good are we?

We will really have to make our mark in Europe after two bad efforts before we can claim to rank among the best. It's a black spot which haunts us, even allowing for the problems of changing the side to fall in line with UEFA's rules counting Welshmen, Scots and the Irish as foreign. But in terms of domestic football I think we are close to matching those who have gone before us. Comparing one era with another is always slightly unreal because there are so many variables.

Bobby Charlton, who played in the successful side of the Sixties with Denis Law and George Best is on record as saying that we are as good as the team of his day, but his old team-mate Willie Morgan begs to differ. Willie says that the overall standard is not as good now. He argues that there were more good teams around in the Sixties and that even their relegated sides were better than the average Premiership team of today. Well, I leave that to the followers of United who have perhaps watched long enough to make their own judgments. I certainly think it is unrealistic to compare us with the Busby Babes because in the Fifties Sir Matt Busby had obviously created an exceptional team which was only just getting into its stride when it was destroyed in the Munich air crash. Who knows what they might have gone on to achieve, because the average age of that team was only around 23.

What I do know is that Alex Ferguson has built something comparable and special which has come together in a superb way. We couldn't wait to get started last season to show that the previous year's success had not just been a flash in the pan. It was basically the same side as the year before, except for one major summer signing, Roy Keane, who had joined us from Nottingham Forest for a record fee of £3.75m. Roy was brought straight into the side to play against Arsenal in the FA Charity Shield and forced Brian McClair on to the substitutes' bench. He was in distinguished company, though, and when you glanced across to the 'reserves' you appreciated the strength in depth at the club. For sitting there, in addition to Brian McClair, were Bryan Robson, Lee Sharpe and Darren Ferguson – a timely reminder that we all faced stiff competition for our places. Robbo was particularly disappointed to miss out because he had done well in pre-season training and thought he had done enough to be in the starting line-up. You could see he was itching to have a go when he came on as a sub for the last 22 minutes and immediately got us organised after we looked in danger of losing.

I was quite satisfied on a personal level after scoring our goal in a 1-1 draw. It came in the ninth minute, a lovely move which saw Cantona steering a cross from Denis Irwin into my path. Ian Wright equalised for the Gunners just before half-time and the scoring stayed that way so we were forced into a penalty shoot-out. The Charity Shield is a nice spectacle, I suppose, and it helps charity but this one was never a classic – and not many of them are. I certainly don't think it is necessary to decide this kind of game with penalty shots. No one seemed very bothered and we were more embarrassed than anything. In my view, the Shield should be shared in the event of a draw. I don't think Robbo was complaining, though, because Wembley had given him the chance to show he was in good nick so that when the serious stuff started in defence of our crown at Norwich he was the replacement for Eric, who had damaged his knee in the Charity game.

Robbo celebrated by scoring a good goal and with a scrambled effort from Ryan Giggs we were off to a good start with a 2-0 win. We played really well, always quicker to the ball, and we were never in any trouble. We carried on in that vein for our first appearance of the season at Old Trafford with Roy Keane marking his home début by scoring twice in a 3-0 win against Sheffield United. It's always an ordeal for an expensive player to appear in front of his own supporters for the first time knowing he has to try and justify his transfer tag. In that position you keep reminding yourself that the fee is nothing to do with you, but it doesn't really work; you know people are expecting you to show you are value for money.

Roy showed his worth all right and made it clear what a tremendous asset he would prove for the Reds. Roy tells me that he turned down a better offer from elsewhere when he left Forest for Old Trafford because he wanted to be with a club which won things. It hasn't worked out too badly for him so far, and as Roy showed in his first outing at Old Trafford, he has played his part in maintaining the momentum of success. He is a forceful character for one so young and he is lively on and off the pitch. We call him Damien, after the devil child in *The Omen*, though I'm not sure he sees the funny side of our nickname for him. I helped with one of Roy's goals and scored the final one myself after Ryan Giggs had left five opponents in his wake on a storming run down the wing.

Then Newcastle came to Old Trafford and made it difficult for us. They were the first team we played last season to set their stall out with the emphasis on stopping us playing while hoping for a breakaway to earn them something. Several teams tried it later on with a certain amount of success. It's an area which the manager says we must work on. Ryan Giggs put us ahead in the first half with a well-flighted free kick, but we were sluggish and we let Andy Cole in for a late equaliser.

The Newcastle striker went on to enjoy a marvellous season, scoring a stack of goals. I certainly rate him highly, though it will be interesting to see whether he can be quite as successful this year. Second time around is always the big test. The manager gave us a bit of a roasting and said we had been careless as well as going into the match thinking it was going to be easy. His words struck home because when we went to Villa Park a couple of days later we were our real selves in what I thought was a cracking match.

It was one of the best games of the season and reflected the fact that it was Aston Villa who had chased us home for the title the previous season. Both teams did well with Paul Ince figuring strongly to help Lee Sharpe score both goals in a 2-1 win. We were all delighted for Lee, back on home territory as a Brummie and back on target after scoring only once in 30 League and Cup games the previous season.

Lee had had a rough couple of seasons, what with meningitis and two hernia operations. At one stage he must have wondered if a promising career was going to remain just that – promising, but without going any further. I think it was in that match that he introduced his hip-shaking celebration dance. It's not my bag, but perhaps I am showing my age and it's something that belongs to the new breed of footballer. I don't think it appealed very much to the boss either because word got round that he had to cut it out. His words seemed to fall on deaf ears, though, because, encouraged by players like Ryan Giggs and Paul Ince, I noticed he still managed the occasional wiggle whenever he scored.

Perhaps Mr Ferguson recalled the tough time Lee had had and relented, and it has been hard for Lee, because not only did he have to work hard for his fitness, he also faced stiff competition for a first-team place. Right through the season there was a fierce rivalry between Lee, Ryan Giggs and Andrei Kanchelskis for the two wing positions. Andrei was the loser for a lot of the time, but he hit such a hot streak towards the end of the season that it was Lee who drew the short straw and was on the bench for the FA Cup final.

They are all terrific players, but I have got to say that when it comes to crossing the ball into the box nice and early and accurately, then I think Sharpey has the edge. Perhaps as a striker this is the aspect of wing play I look for and I accept that when it comes to running at opponents and getting into the box themselves then perhaps the other two have the advantage. Anyway, it's a super situation for the manager and gives him options. The other factor in the equation is that Lee is no mean full-back. He started his senior career there and it's a useful ploy for Europe – says he, knowing that if Denis Irwin, an Irishman, is left out then Welshman Hughes has more chance of staying in the team!

I don't think Lee is too happy about playing too many games at full-back, but that's the manager's problem. What I do know is that the Villa result and performance seemed to confirm that we were in serious contention for the Championship again and we confirmed it in the next two fix-tures, with a 3-1 win at Southampton and a 3-0 home victory over West Ham.

After recovering from injury, Eric Cantona made his first League appearance of the season at The Dell, and quickly made up for lost time by scoring with a delightful chip over the head of Tim Flowers from the tightest of angles. Lee Sharpe and Denis Irwin scored the other goals in a display which I think sent a few ripples through the Premiership. Ian Branfoot, the Saints manager, went on record saying that he fancied us for the Championship and we certainly began to feel that we were capable of hanging on to the title.

The next game saw me dropped, and I was not a happy man. The boss told me he had to get the team in shape for our opening tie in the European Cup and that he would be trying out a few things in the two League fixtures before playing against Honved in Budapest. I didn't seem to be missed against the Hammers as Lee took his goal tally to four in three games to go with a penalty from Eric and a late goal from Steve Bruce. My second game out saw us lose our first match of the season with a 1–0 defeat at Chelsea. I wouldn't claim it was because of my absence; more likely it was down to the midweek internationals, which had seen a lot of our team travelling far and wide. Someone said we had 11 players involved in eight teams in World Cup qualifiers. The manager reckoned that we looked shattered and that our defeat was the price we paid for the heavy international calls.

Gavin Peacock scored the only goal of the afternoon, and though Eric had gone close with a clever lob which went over the goalkeeper only to hit the bar, we couldn't really complain about the result on the run of the play. It hadn't been a bad opening burst, with only one point dropped out of six games before the trip to Chelsea. The manager said we had the experience to get over it and after beating the Hungarians at Old Trafford we returned to our winning ways in the Championship with a blistering run of eight successive wins.

It was a busy period, with European ties and the start of the Coca-Cola Cup occupying midweek slots, but the League was always our priority and we kept up a pretty hot pace. A 1–0 win against Arsenal at Old Trafford was useful because the

Gunners were our nearest challengers at the time and were strongly fancied by those who thought successive Championships would be too hard a task for us. I enjoyed the game, possibly because I was back in the side. Neither manager reckoned much to the quality of the game, with our boss saying it was difficult to decide which team was the more tired.

Steve Bruce gave a typical performance and showed why he was the obvious choice to take over as captain whenever Bryan Robson was absent. He had to go off for three stitches in a head wound after a clash of heads, but came back to continue to throw his bandaged head at the ball. I know they say that where there is no sense there is no feeling, but he really did have a marvellous season. I hope I don't upset him if I say he hasn't quite got the touch of a Cantona or Giggs, but he more than makes up for it with his commitment. And do you recall that astounding season in 1991 when he was United's third highest scorer?

A lot of his goals were penalties, 11 to be exact, and it should have been 12 because he missed one, but he still grabbed eight goals from normal play and set-pieces, which isn't bad. His total of 19 was only two behind Brian McClair, who shared top spot with me on 21 apiece. Steve is always good for half a dozen, which means he can give his partner, Gary Pallister, some terrible stick because goal-scoring is not the big man's forte – something like one a season!

Coming back up to date, though, my own scoring had left a lot to be desired, with only a couple of goals under my belt by mid-September and I was anxious to boost my own total. I came to life in the next two League games, which saw me knock in four: two against Swindon and two at Sheffield Wednesday. We were three up against Swindon but took our foot off the pedal to allow them back into the game. I got a second goal to give us a 4-2 scoreline and I always felt we had a couple of gears in reserve.

The game at Hillsborough was much closer. Wednesday scored first, and though I got my pair, with one from Ryan as well, they grabbed a late score to see us hanging on anxiously. Perhaps we suffered another hangover from a midweek European tie. It came out right in the end, though. Sheffield Wednesday used to have the Indian sign on us but I think we have turned it right round now and we continued on our merry winning way.

We then had a fortnight's break between League fixtures filled by a Coca-Cola Cup tie against Stoke and a round of World Cup qualifiers which saw Andrei Kanchelskis return as just about the only happy international and the rest of us, bar the Republic of Ireland, heading for failure. Alex Ferguson was worried we would let World Cup disappointment affect our club form but we got it together against Spurs to win 2-1 with goals from Roy Keane and Lee Sharpe. It wasn't a classic, but Ossie Ardiles said afterwards that if the rest of them were not careful Manchester United could run away with the Championship. He said he couldn't see who was going to stop us and Howard Kendall agreed with him after our next win, when we went to Everton to extract a 1-0 victory in what was possibly our worst performance of the season.

Everton deserved a draw on the day, though there was no denying the quality of Lee Sharpe's goal, a volley from just outside the box which flew past Neville Southall like the pro-verbial rocket. The Everton manager said he rated it as a contender for goal of the season. It was Lee's sixth League goal in nine games and it gave us a nine-point lead at the top of the table after only two months of the season. What was perhaps even more encouraging was that in that match we picked up three points without really playing all that well, always a good sign!

At this stage of the season we couldn't seem to go wrong. In the next game, for instance, QPR came to Old Trafford to take the lead and give us a chasing. Ray Wilkins, a nice bloke who helped me settle into the United team when he was a Red, didn't look 37 as he ran the match from midfield. Our governor wasn't a happy man at the interval and we put on a much better second-half performance to pull the game out of the fire. Eric got a good goal to equalise and I got the winner. It was a scruffy goal, not the kind I'm supposed to score, so there was even more satisfaction for me.

This reputation I have for scoring spectacular goals rather than run-of-the-mill jobs − and I have to admit that I don't pick up many goals which are bread-and-butter for many strikers − is one which irritates me. The reason is not that I am too proud and can't be bothered to hunt down the tap-ins, I assure you. I believe there is a quite ordinary explanation linked with the way I play, coming deep to share in the build-up. It means that if I am involved in setting up play it is very difficult to get myself into the goalmouth before the ball. A poacher or sniffer of goals hangs around the six-yard box, and you don't often find him dropping back to take part in the approach play.

So you pay your money and take your choice about which kind of striker you want. What you can't do is have it both ways, which is why I was pleased to pick up the short-range effort which won us a match on the day Gary Pallister missed his only League game of the season.

The win put us in good mood for our European Cup second leg against Galatasaray, a game involving a nightmare trip to Istanbul which didn't work out the way we wanted, but I'll come to that later. At least in the League we were still going from strength to strength and underlined the point by winning the Maine Road derby 3-2 in an amazing game. The Manchester City fans gave us the works before kick-off, pelting us with bars of Turkish Delight to rub in our Galatasaray disaster.

And when we went off at half-time with the Blues holding a two-goal lead I am sure the home supporters had visions of giving us a 5-1 drubbing similar to their victory in 1989-90. Niall Quinn had scored both goals and given us all kinds of trouble, but it was, happily for us, a different story in the second half. Eric played a very significant part in turning the game round. He started to drop deeper and the tactic threw City into confusion. At the same time we improved the accuracy of our passing and in the end City just couldn't get the ball off us.

It was an amazingly cool display by the Frenchman after his traumatic experience in Turkey. Not only did he cause havoc, but he scored two goals to bring us level with just 13 minutes remaining. I think our opponents were groggy by then and it was no great surprise when Roy Keane came steaming through to blast home a cross from Denis Irwin to give us victory. If we had gone down at Maine Road after Istanbul it really would have capped an awful week. As it was, we were up and running again and well prepared for a visit from the Wimbledon Crazy Gang.

I have a grudging respect for Wimbledon and their approach to the game. When we first started going to Plough Lane, a pocket-sized ground with pretty basic facilities, it was quite a culture shock, and, of course, Vinnie Jones and company played on that fact in an effort to unsettle the more sophisticated clubs.

People couldn't believe it but they always seemed to find an edge when they played us because we are the type of team they love to beat. We have had a few run-ins over the years, notably the infamous tunnel incident which featured John Fashanu and saw our Viv Anderson knocked out cold. Then there was the season they came to Old Trafford and won. There was no holding them as Vinnie marched up and down the corridor smoking a big cigar while their huge team ghetto-blaster threatened to take the roof off.

Actually, Wimbledon are not as bad as they once were. They play a better class of football at Selhurst Park and they have left a lot of their excesses at Plough Lane. They have lost some of their wild impact and at the same time we have grown used to them. Now when they have their music blaring out, we simply ask them to play something we know! Anyway, they didn't present us with much of a problem on this occasion, which was more notable for Gary Pallister scoring his only goal of the season, and with a header.

The big man gets up well enough in defence, but we always tease him when he comes up front with us for corners and free kicks and ask him how it is that he is 6 ft 4 ins but jumps as if he is 5 ft 4 ins! Anyway, he got us off to a good start and, though Fashanu headed an equaliser, I scored and Andrei Kanchelskis got a third goal for a comfortable win. I have got to hand it to Wimbledon: if you beat them they can take it and they will give you both respect and credit. That, of course, doesn't stop them milking it when they finish on top. Personally, I don't have any problem with their physical approach. You know what to expect when you play against Vinnie Jones and there is certainly nothing devious about the man. I think Fashanu got away with a lot playing for Wimbledon and it will be interesting to see how he fares at a higher-profile club now he has joined Aston Villa.

It was our eighth successive League win and it had to end sometime, even if it was a bit of a surprise to find that Ipswich were the team which halted our march in a goalless game at Old Trafford. They came to stop us playing and their game plan worked to perfection. Overall, I don't think such tactics get you very far and, indeed, they narrowly escaped relegation. They worked hard for their point against us, though, and it was the first time we had failed to score at Old Trafford for over a year. At the end of the day, the onus is on us to find the answer to a negative approach. On this occasion it didn't do us any real damage. Other results went our way and we, in fact, found ourselves increasing our lead to 12 points.

We got back on the winning track at Coventry when

Eric scored his tenth goal of the season. Peter Schmeichel helped us with a great double save against Mick Quinn but it was the start of a slightly sticky patch which saw us drop points, with more drawn games than we would have wished for. Norwich held us to 2–2 at Old Trafford. Chris Sutton gave us a glimpse of the power that put him in the frame for his big transfer by scoring, but we went off at the interval leading 2–1 with goals from Giggs and McClair. Norwich got their equaliser at the start of the second half with a harsh penalty. We were still 12 points clear at the top of the table, though, and we went 15 points ahead a few days later with a 3–0 win at Sheffield United. I scored after 12 minutes and with other goals from Sharpey and Oo-ah Cantona we were never in trouble. Ladbrokes closed their books on us winning the Championship, while Manchester bookmakers Done Brothers announced they would take bets on how many points we would win the title by!

Newcastle pegged us back a little with a 1–1 draw at St James's Park. Kevin Keegan had done his best to put us on edge with a war of words. He called on the rest of Britain to back his team in an effort to keep us in reach at the top of the table. Paul Ince answered him by getting his first goal of the season but Andy Cole probably did justice to the scoreline with a late equaliser to give him the remarkable return of 17 league goals in 19 appearances. It was Cole who had got the Newcastle equaliser at Old Trafford in August and he proved the thorn in our side again in this match. After the game Keegan put his finger on our strength. He said: 'I looked at the Manchester United bench and saw Roy Keane and Andrei Kanchelskis waiting to come on with Bryan Robson sitting in the stand.' It's a great advantage to have such talented depth in the squad that you can afford to leave such top-class players on the sidelines. Unfortunately, I had to come off early with a recurrence of a heel injury that was starting to become a problem.

We reached the halfway mark in the Premiership programme with a 3-1 win against Aston Villa at Old Trafford.
We had totalled 52 points, which was really an astonishing
figure and raised the possibility of breaking all records with a
century of points. The performance against Villa suggested it
was possible, though I accept that the scoreline perhaps flattered us slightly. Cantona had scored after 22 minutes but the
other three goals in the game all came during injury time. Eric
scored again and so did Paul Ince, with a little help from me.
Villa joined in the scoring rush but we were home and dry by
then and ready for a testing run of fixtures over Christmas and
the New Year.

Chapter Three

THE GOVERNOR

PAUL INCE is the team joker. He never stops talking, he's hyperactive and to say he gets on everyone's nerves is being kind to him! Then when he starts to score goals he becomes unbearable and there is just no stopping him. The young players like his bounce and bubble and find a ready response. Naturally enough it's Paul that the likes of Ryan Giggs and Lee Sharpe run to for their hip-shaking dances to celebrate a goal and if there is any larking about in the dressing-room at the training ground you can be sure our chirpy Cockney will not be far from the action.

The fire extinguishers at the Cliff, our training ground, have never been used so much since Paul and Ryan started to clown around in our lighter moments. Actually, Incey likes to be called the Governor. Nicknames run right through the club but because he likes to hear us refer to him like that we go the other way and simply call him Paul. It drives him mad.

It's all good fun of course and has a part to play in team spirit, but I can tell you there is no one more serious or ambitious than the Governor once the action starts. In my view, Paul has been our most consistent player over the last two or three seasons. He's forceful, quick and strong and if his delay in signing a new contract at United was anything to do with moving abroad, I hope it won't be for some time yet. He is an important part of Manchester United as he demonstrated particularly in the second half of our historic League and Cup double last season.

Blackburn Rovers were the team which made us sweat for the Championship on the last lap, but when we met them at Christmas they were 14 points behind us, lying in third place. They had had a modest start to the season and though Alan Shearer was scoring freely I don't think I really saw them as our main rivals. If we looked over our shoulders at all it was to see how Leeds were faring.

They did, however, give us a glimpse of things to come when they came to Old Trafford on Boxing Day and held us to a 1-1 draw on our own ground. They scored early in the game through Kevin Gallacher and it wasn't until the last minute that Incey managed to preserve an unbeaten home record which had now stretched to 14 months. We were slack in the early stages and Kevin Gallacher didn't meet much of a challenge when he ran through to put the visitors ahead. Paul saved the day by scoring his third goal in three games. As an attacking midfield player, he knows he should perhaps get more goals and it is a bit of a mystery that he doesn't, though I've got to acknowledge that his total of eight in the League last season was a big improvement and a very valuable contribution. It certainly was in this match, and as usual there was no holding him.

I went off early again in the Blackburn game with my heel bothering me and I missed the next three League games. The boys obviously didn't miss me at Oldham where they romped to a 5-2 win. I would love to have been in the next match, on New Year's Day, when Leeds were the visitors and surprised us by looking as if they were content with a draw. The game was goalless and frustrating. Leeds, at that point, were still in with a chance of catching us and I thought they would have been more ambitious. Still, from their perspective, I suppose an away draw at Old Trafford is perhaps a good result. Yet this was our fourth home draw in five League games and our points lead was starting to be nibbled away.

The next game was drawn as well but you could hardly say there was anything defensive or negative about it. We took a three-goal lead and then came home from Anfield with a 3-3 draw. Our scoring was incredible with Bruce, Giggs and Irwin all hitting the target in the first 23 minutes. Giggsy was in blinding form and his goal was a beauty. Liverpool hit back with two goals from Nigel Clough followed by a late equaliser from Neil Ruddock. It was Fantasy Football and I don't think the manager knew whether to laugh or cry at the end. He described it as a once-in-a-lifetime match and I wish I'd been there.

I played in a couple of Cup ties before returning to the League side at Tottenham and scoring my tenth League goal of the season to give us a 1-0 win. I enjoyed my near-post flick from Roy Keane's cross but the day belonged to Eric Cantona, who produced a masterly performance on a muddy and bumpy pitch. Steve Bruce played despite a cracked rib, displaying typical courage and tenacity.

Then came a day of great emotion, the first match following the death of Sir Matt Busby. It was difficult to get into the mood for football on such a sad occasion. I think all our thoughts were more on the great man's achievements than on our scrap against Everton. Although none of us played for him, we are all aware that this was the man who built Manchester United and laid the foundations for the club we know today. The mood was set right at the start when a lone piper led out the two teams. It was a haunting, melancholic lament. We seemed to be kept for an age in the tunnel while the packed ground waited in hushed silence. The reason for the delay, I think, was that the piper was so overcome by the occasion that he had difficulty catching enough breath to inflate the bag on his bagpipes. He had to walk up and down to recover his composure, but all the time the supporters of both teams kept a respectful hush. There is little love lost between Scousers and Mancs but the Everton fans were fantastic. Sir Matt would have enjoyed the match. It was almost as if the players of both teams made a special effort to bring out all that is good in the game and it was uncanny that Ryan Giggs, a young player carrying the torch for the Busby Babes, should have had a particularly good match.

I can't say I knew Sir Matt. I didn't see a lot of him but when you went upstairs to the office at Old Trafford and walked down the corridor you would invariably see him sitting behind his office desk. He kept his door open all the time and would cheerfully wave at you with his pipe in his hand and a big smile on his face. That open, friendly approach seems to have been a big part of the man throughout his life. We were all pleased that we had won the Championship in his last full season with us and of all the photographs taken around that time the one that stands out was taken when we actually clinched the title. Sir Matt was standing there with a big smile on his face as he looked round the ground, his ground really.

Few players actually wanted to play that day because the ghosts of matches past were never far away but afterwards we were all glad we had shared the experience and it was fitting that Ryan was the scorer in our 1-0 win.

We ran into a busy spell involving ties in both the FA Cup and Coca-Cola Cup competitions, but, unlike the season two years previously, we maintained reasonable impetus in the League. We went to QPR, for instance, sandwiched between four Cup games but completed a League double to the tune of 3-2. Andrei and Eric, two of our foreign legion, saw us leading 2-1 at half-time before Ryan stole the show with a scintillating goal which involved beating at least two opponents.

So how good is Ryan – is he really better than George Best?

I am not trying to dodge the issue but my reply is that he is as good as he wants to be. By that I mean he is really only at the dawn of his career. He hasn't achieved what Best did. I didn't see the Irishman in the flesh myself, but glimpses on film and enthusiastic tales from supporters make it clear that he was a special player. Ryan has the football world at his feet. He has all the natural attributes: quick, great feet and he is brave with it. For his age, he is mature and streetwise. When I got into the first team around his age I was a relative innocent. Ryan seems to know what it's all about and, as I say, it's all a matter of whether he can build on his early success, and that's something which is down to him.

Alex Ferguson has helped him by keeping the media off his back. Because it was obvious he was something special, he became something of a cult figure and there's nothing the press, television and radio like better. He was shielded from giving too many interviews. When you are young it is easy to put your foot in it and say all the wrong things. Now the wraps are coming off and he can handle it. I wonder whether keeping the media at bay has added an air of mystery to him, although in football terms he is the hottest property in the game. I think he will keep his feet on the ground. He has a group of close friends and though he is seen around some of the trendy night spots, there is nothing wrong in that at his age as a single man. I'm sure he will come through the temptations.

The game against QPR was our 30th in all competitions without defeat, a record for United and one better than the Busby Babes in 1956. We drew the next League game 2-2 at West Ham. We didn't defend very well and the Londoners raised their game. In the circumstances, it was a good result because I have never seen a player take as much abuse as Paul Ince experienced on returning to his old club. The London fans gave him a really torrid time. They booed every time he touched the ball and threw bananas on to the pitch. Before the match, there had been threats of violence and all because some of the club's fans considered him a traitor for leaving to join Manchester United.

They chanted 'Judas' on his first return to Upton Park following his transfer four years previously. He was understandably nervous at first but he had promised he wouldn't hide and he was there at the very end to rifle a cross from Roy Keane into the goal and down the throats of his tormentors. It was a valuable point and I was pleased with my early goal as well.

All unbeaten runs come to an end some time, though I confess it came as a shock to find Chelsea our conquerors for a second time and Gavin Peacock once again the scorer of the goal in a repeat 1-0 win for the Londoners. If we are looking for excuses, we had just played in the Coca-Cola Cup semi-final to reach Wembley so perhaps there was a touch of complacency in our approach, though we had plenty of possession. Eric was missing, but he hadn't been at Hillsborough in midweek either and it hadn't made any difference then. The biggest factor for me was that Chelsea exploited our weakness when confronted by a team playing with a lot of men behind the ball. We often seem to get bogged down and then prove vulnerable to the break, and Peacock is a specialist at running dangerously from deep positions.

He hit us this time in the 64th minute and then the Londoners really shut up shop to keep us out. Other than encourage Blackburn, it didn't do us any harm, in the sense that we hit back hard to win an FA Cup quarter-final against Charlton and then romped to our biggest League win of the season with a 5-1 victory against Sheffield Wednesday at Old Trafford. I think the Wednesday players were maybe thinking more of summer holidays. Their season was over, whereas we still had a lot to play for and we went for it with two goals from Eric and one apiece from myself, Ryan and Paul Ince. The goalkeeper had a bit of a nightmare, I must add! It was very easy and gave no inkling of the storm about to burst round our heads with four sendings-off in five games.

I must confess that the bare facts make it look as though we had suddenly gone berserk. Perhaps we were getting a little strung up as we looked over our shoulders at Blackburn and wondered about the last lap, though it never felt to me as if the team had the jitters. I think it was just an unfortunate series of incidents which came all at once.

The first dismissal had come in the Cup tie against Charlton before the Sheffield Wednesday game. Peter Schmeichel had come rushing out of goal and out of the penalty area to stop Kim Grant, who had broken through on his own. To this day I'm not exactly sure which of the two offences earned Peter the red card. It was perhaps for handling outside the area or it may have been for the fact that he also took the man. Referee Rob Hart didn't seem to have any doubts and Les Sealey made a rare first-team appearance in the second half with Paul Parker the man pulled off to make way for our substitute goalkeeper.

There was talk of an appeal, but Peter's plight was over-shadowed when our Frenchman got himself sent off twice in successive matches. When Eric kicks over the traces there are no half-measures and, to be frank, there was not a lot we could say in his defence when he was sent off at Swindon for 'stamp-ing' on an opponent.

Eric was the first to admit after the match that he had been in the wrong, though I have got to say that he had been seriously provoked — in fact, we all had. Swindon were stuck at the bottom of the table and they had clearly decided that if they couldn't match our skill they would see if they could literally knock us out of our stride.

They got stuck in, just like Wimbledon of the old days, and we didn't get a lot of protection from the referee, Brian Hill. We were disappointed with our performance, though it had looked to be OK when Roy Keane headed in a centre from me which gave us an early lead. Swindon equalised with a long-range deflected shot but we nosed in front again with a goal from Paul. But then in the 65th minute came Eric's clash with John Moncur, who had kept his legs wrapped round our man as he lay on the ground. Eric, struggling to break free, did so and as he moved off gave the Swindon player a dig in the ribs with his foot.

It was certainly not stamping in the Rugby Union sense, when players finish up with heads split open and lines gouged by studs across their backs. I doubt if Moncur was marked. Certainly, Eric had to go for his early bath, but it was not vicious or as bad as the uproar in the media implied. The worst part, of course, was that we were left a man short for the last 25 minutes and Swindon steamed in for an equaliser from Jan Fjortoft for a 2-2 draw and we dropped two points.

I might add that Swindon could thank their lucky stars that the Cantona controversy switched the spotlight away from the fact that I was punched by one of the home fans. I was chasing a ball as it went out of play and was nudged by an opponent so that I went off the pitch as well to finish up at the fence in front of the Swindon supporters. One of them immediately took a swing and clipped me on the side of the head. I refrained from making a meal of it, but really it was quite a serious offence for a visiting player to be struck by a fan. Because of all the fuss about Eric, it was completely over-looked by the media and Swindon went unpunished.

But if people were throwing up their hands in horror at the Frenchman's behaviour, it was nothing compared with the meal they made of the next fixture when Eric was sent off again. This time at Arsenal, Cantona went off for two yellow cards. No one quarrelled with the first booking, but the second was the result of a baying crowd and a tense atmosphere. As I saw it, Eric and Tony Adams both went charging into a mêlée of players and at the last moment Eric tried to jump out of the way. Referee Vic Callow obviously considered Eric was guilty of dangerous play and booked him, but we felt he had been unlucky, particularly when we realised that, as it was his second dismissal of the season, he would be banned for five matches, a stiff price to pay indeed.

Eric wasn't the end of our disciplinary problems, as Roy Keane earned a caution at Highbury, which meant he would be serving a one-match ban for the FA Cup semi-final. We drew 2-2 with Arsenal and saw our lead further nibbled away. We had led twice, both goals coming from Lee Sharpe on his return to the first team after an absence of nearly three months. It was a storming comeback after injury and I was delighted to help him for both goals after benefiting in the past from Lee's enterprising work on the wing.

The next match brought us to our lowest ebb of the season. We lost the Coca-Cola Cup final against Aston Villa, which, when added to a run of five League games with only one win plus our disciplinary troubles, saw the critics at our throats. We were wobbling, people said, and according to them it was going to be a repeat of two seasons earlier when we failed to stay the course and were beaten into second place by Leeds United. Incidentally, it was the game at Wembley which brought us our fourth sending-off in five games with the luckless Andrei Kanchelskis penalised for stopping a goal-bound shot from Dalian Atkinson with his arm.

Andrei realised it was a penalty, but was mortified to discover he must also leave the field. I have never seen anyone look so baffled but the rules say that a deliberate hand-ball in those circumstances should be punished with an automatic dismissal. I think even referee Keith Cooper was embarrassed and apologised for what he was about to do! But though this was a technical sending-off, rather than the result of violent play, it didn't stop our critics adding it to the disciplinary black-list to suggest we were cracking up and losing our cool.

We certainly had some tough matches coming up, especially a showdown with Blackburn on our rivals' ground at Ewood Park. At least, though, we gave ourselves some breathing space by beating Liverpool 1-0 at Old Trafford to put us in a better frame of mind for the head-to-head with Rovers. On that occasion Paul Ince was our hero with his third League goal in four games, glancing in a first-half header from Lee Sharpe's corner. Liverpool had a lot of possession and their manager, Roy Evans, claimed they deserved to win, but they lacked pace and never really opened us up. I had a hard match against Neil Ruddock and didn't know what had hit me at one point, but it was a good battle and we all felt in better shape for the trip to Blackburn.

We fancied ourselves to win and put our challengers back in their place but we came a right cropper and were well beaten 2-0. There could be no argument about the fairness of the result because Blackburn were the better team on the day. They were stronger than us and Alan Shearer demonstrated his remarkable scoring ability by grabbing both goals to take his season's tally to 29 in 33 appearances.

Personally, I found it hard to tune in mentally. As their ground was undergoing redevelopment, we had to change in one place, away from the ground, and then catch a bus to another room nearer the pitch. It threw our normal routine and our defeat certainly left the Championship wide open with Blackburn on our shoulders, just three points behind. So much for our January lead of 14 points and the bookies refusing to take any more bets on us for the title.

Shearer did his best for his team after the match as well by throwing out his 'bottle' challenge. We were already concerned, too, that it had been our first match in the run-in without the suspended Cantona, just another of the factors nibbling at our confidence as we waited for the arrival of

Oldham, on paper a pushover as a team in fear of relegation, but traditionally capable of springing a few surprises at the last gasp when they have their backs to the wall.

Ryan scored an early goal but an equaliser from Sean McCarthy had us wobbling until Dion Dublin came on as a substitute and grabbed a goal. Incey scored just a minute later. Oldham pulled back a late goal, but really we had polished them off to stay three points clear at the top of the table, and as Oldham boss Joe Royle summed up: 'I called United awesome in the game at Boundary Park. They weren't quite that in this match, but you cannot be awesome for 42 matches. Teams which can get winning results when they are not at their best are the ones which win things. United are still a great side.'

We had to play Oldham again in the FA Cup semi-final, and while we were happy to win through to Wembley we weren't so pleased to find that, during our absence from the League, Blackburn had drawn level on points. The pressure was mounting, particularly when we made a mess of it at Wimbledon to come home beaten 1-0. Peter Schmeichel, troubled by an ankle injury, made a rare mistake with a low cross which let John Fashanu in for an early goal. I think they were more surprised than us and they immediately got every-one behind the ball to hang on to their lead.

Blackburn had lost as well, which was some consolation, but at the same time it flashed across my mind that perhaps we might not win the title again after all. The fact that we had missed a great opportunity of going three points clear worried me. It was the only time I ever doubted, but even then it was only a flash of fear; it was never a worry gnawing away. It was a warning, though, that we would have to pull ourselves together, and, inspired by Eric Cantona's return from suspension, we did exactly that to launch into a run of four wins which squeezed the pips out of Blackburn and saw us take the title by eight points.

It didn't look as easy as that, though, as we waited for the Old Trafford derby and wondered what such a long ban might have done to our temperamental Frenchman. It was, in fact, a needless worry and it was City who looked jittery in the opening stages when Paul Walsh and Uwe Rossler both missed good chances to open the scoring. I was pleased with my contribution. I got Andrei away down the right for Eric to score from his cross in the 40th minute, and a couple of minutes later I put Eric through to shoot past Andy Dibble. What a spectacular return from suspension: two goals in a derby, which knocked the stuffing out of the Blues to win us the match 2-0.

It left us two points ahead with a game in hand. Assuming Blackburn won their remaining three games, it meant we had to win two and draw one from four fixtures to keep our crown. Now the pressure was really piling up on Blackburn, while we were playing with a refreshed appetite, all those woes and worries of the previous month firmly banished.

The next game really posed problems. All matches with Leeds in recent seasons have been fierce, and though the players of both clubs get on well with each other, there is so much bitterness, even hatred, between the two sets of supporters that it is worrying. I think Leeds have taken over from Liverpool as the number-one object of hate among our fans, while the Leeds crowd shout terrible obscenities at us, with most of their venom focussed on Cantona. The treatment Paul Ince received at West Ham is nothing compared to what Eric has to endure when he plays against his old club.

The old fox doesn't let it upset him, though, and he played his usual thoughtful game at Elland Road in a match which brought me some good reviews. I must say, I felt good and I was delighted to give Andrei a return pass for the first goal. Near the end I worked a similar move for Ryan to score and complete a 2-0 win after what I consider our best performance of the season. Given the circumstances, I thought we really turned it on and it was somehow fitting that both goals should have been scored by the wingers because throughout the season we operated well on the flanks, producing a pattern of play which made us good to watch. After the second goal our fans burst into a spontaneous chant of 'champions', and they know the game. It was at this point that we knew nothing could stop us keeping our title crown.

We got our heads down at Ipswich to come up with a 2-1 win. I guess it wasn't a pretty match and we looked to be up against it when Peter Schmeichel, struggling with his bad ankle again, fumbled a shot from Ian Marshall for Chris Kiwomya to score. Peter limped off after half an hour to bring Gary Walsh on for his first taste of League football in two years. We all know what a good goalkeeper he is, though, and we kept our cool to dig out a winning result, with goals from Eric and Ryan.

It might sound trivial, but we all thought Ipswich had let the grass grow longer than usual in an effort to put us off our passing game. Something had us struggling, though, and it was some time before we settled down to our usual game. Yet it was significant that we got back into the match after going a goal down, not always a feature of our side.

After that win it was difficult to avoid winning the Championship. Blackburn must have felt it was all up, and indeed it was when they went to Coventry and lost. We were champions again with two games to spare. While some of the players went round to Steve Bruce's house to celebrate, the manager went on record as saying he would rather we had won it playing a game. I know what he meant, but secretly I think the overwhelming feeling was relief that it was finally all over and we had pulled off the difficult coup of winning successive Championships.

At least we tried to play like the champions we had become when Southampton came to Old Trafford. It was difficult to strike a balance between finding an edge and doing our duty while celebrating our success. We managed it reasonably well in the face of some spirited play by the Saints. Andrei, who had made the right-wing position his own in the closing stages of the season to give him the confidence to sign a new contract to stay at Old Trafford, celebrated by scoring his tenth goal of the season, and I was able to add a late score courtesy of my partner, Oo-ah, who had helped me to hit the big-time again in front of goal.

The Saints gave our defence a busy afternoon and tested Gary Walsh in his first full appearance of the season. Gary had been in the shadows for the best part of five years, fighting to overcome various injuries. He stepped up as if he had never been away and so impressed the manager that Les Sealey has been allowed to leave to join Blackpool. Gary now takes over the understudy role to Schmeichel and the Dane knows he faces a challenge for his place.

We wound up the League season by playing Coventry at home. Perhaps by then our minds were more on the FA Cup final the following week, because we could only play out a goalless draw. Mind you, that didn't stop a few players striving might and main to do well. One in particular was the never-say-die Bryan Robson, who was making his farewell appearance before joining Middlesbrough.

A few of us were rested. My heel was playing up again and Alex Ferguson took the opportunity of giving Giggs, Kanchelskis and Ince a break. Keane was on the bench but was brought on for the last quarter of an hour so that Bryan could play up front and endeavour to score his 100th goal for United. The boys bent over backwards trying to put him in for one last goal, but it wasn't to be. Still, as the manager said afterwards, the skipper doesn't need a century to register his place in the history of Old Trafford. Over the years he has done plenty to assure his ranking among the legends. Even in his last season, with Keane and Ince occupying the main midfield roles, Robbo still managed to make easily enough appearances to win a second Championship medal, and I'm glad he played to the age of 37 to add those gongs to his considerable collection.

At that final game at Old Trafford we were presented with the Premiership trophy – and that really was what it was all about that day before we set off in a bid to make it a League and FA Cup double.

Chapter Four

DREAM TEAM

AT home you might find him playing the piano, and for such a big man he displays a surprisingly delicate touch. At the football ground he makes music of a very different sort and it's difficult to imagine that Peter Schmeichel is the son of a Polish academic who was expected to follow in his father's footsteps as a professional musician and teacher.

Peter has emerged as the most dominant goalkeeper in English football. It's easy to forget that when he signed from Brondby he had been playing in a very different kind of football. Most Danish players are part-timers, and, although he subsequently hit the headlines with his superb performances to help Denmark win the European Championship in 1992, I think a few of us wondered early on just how he would fare in the English game. After playing against Wimbledon at Plough Lane at the start of his career in England, he actually confessed to something of a culture shock. I might add that no one expressed any doubts to his face. He is a huge man and, with his crew–cut, spiky, blond hair, not the kind you'd want to get into an argument with.

Mind you, he does seem to get into some fierce verbal exchanges with Steve Bruce and the other defenders from time to time during matches. Fans must have noted and wondered about these altercations and what exactly they were saying. I've wondered myself and, to be quite honest, I couldn't really tell you because it seems to me they are just making a lot of noise. I think they just shout anything that comes into their heads – it's their way of maintaining concentration and geeing each other up. Our great Dane is very ambitious and very determined, as well as artistic, and we were all delighted when a few months ago he decided to sign on again for the Reds because he had become an important player as we pressed on in the FA Cup in pursuit of the Double.

People are now calling us the dream team and certainly it is the best I have ever played in. In my time at United, the only period to rival the present has been in Ron Atkinson's spell as manager, when we made a remarkable start to season 1985-86 and won our first ten League games. It was my last season before setting sail for Spain and a new life with Barcelona. The second half of the season was the pits for me personally and also to some extent for the rest of the team because, after promising so much, we lost our grip and finished fourth in the League with no compensation from the Cup competitions.

But for the first three months of the season we couldn't do a thing wrong and it wasn't until November that we suffered our first defeat. We opened with a superb 4-0 win against Aston Villa at Old Trafford. I scored twice and went on hitting the target regularly to claim ten goals in the first 14 games. Then, when we lost at Sheffield Wednesday on 9 November, it all started to go wrong. My goal-scoring dried up and we slowly disintegrated. We just did not have the strength in depth and we couldn't cope with injuries and a loss of form in one or two positions.

Now, it's a different story. Although we were relatively untroubled by injury last season, we are stronger all round, which is why we were able to take the two domestic Cup competitions in our stride as well as maintain a hot pace in the Championship race. We reached two finals, winning one of them to complete our League and FA Cup double for the first time in the history of Manchester United. That all-round performance tells you the level we have reached. The season before, when we won the Championship the first time, we were knocked out early in both the Cups and the season before that, 1992–93, when we progressed on two Cup fronts and went the distance to Wembley in the Rumbelows, we found we couldn't keep up our winning ways in the League and we finished runners-up.

This last year, though, we scorched along on all fronts, although our opening third-round tie in the FA Cup gave little indication that we were to go all the way. The bookmakers offered a miserly 12-1 on us for a League and Cup treble but I doubt many would have been tempted had they seen us struggle to beat Sheffield United 1-0 at Bramall Lane. The Sheffield side were down among the dead men in the League and didn't seem to have much confidence in themselves. The level of the game seemed to be set after about four minutes, when we were all caught up pushing and shoving each other in an incident involving Peter Schmeichel and Chris Kamara. It was a bit of a nothing game on a sticky pitch which made passing the ball difficult.

The saving grace for me was that it was my goal which won the match and, even if I say it myself, it was a good one. Half the team seemed to be involved in the build-up and I struck it well. The finish involved an exchange of passes with Paul Ince before I stuck the ball past Alan Kelly. Unfortunately, I managed to take the gloss off by losing my temper and taking a kick at David Tuttle. I felt I had taken a lot of stick without much protection from the referee and I'm afraid I simply lost control. I was on edge because it was the start of my nagging heel injury and I had had only a couple of training sessions in the period leading up to the Cup tie. The dismissal cost me an appearance in a Coca-Cola Cup tie but at least I was available for the FA Cup fourth round at Norwich.

We expected a tough match and that's exactly how it turned out. But Lady Luck smiled on us – especially on Eric, who upset the home fans when he caught John Polston on the shoulder with a back-flick from his boot. Shades of things to come at Swindon later in the season! Our controversial star picked up a booking for another incident but got away with this one without being seen by the referee. He then added insult to injury for Norwich supporters by scoring our second goal in a 2-0 win.

Incidentally, this was the match that saw the boss tangle with Jimmy Hill and end up calling him a 'prat'. The Cup tie was on live television and the BBC pundit had been extremely critical of Eric's behaviour, seemingly incensed that the Frenchman had escaped being punished. He was very outspoken and when one of the press reporters told our manager what had been said on the telly he immediately hit back in equally vitriolic terms. Nothing came of the incident. I think everyone felt it was best forgotten. The boss is always at great pains to protect his players from the press but sometimes it seems as if we should be protecting him. When he has a go, he doesn't half put his foot in it sometimes, especially if he is challenged immediately after a match when he is still excited and all het up.

The first goal had come midway through the first half from Roy Keane, after Giggsy had produced a great run down his wing. It was a timely goal for Roy because there had been a few mutterings that he was not living up to his record transfer tag of £3.75m. It's true that after a bright start to his Old Trafford career he had seemed to lose his way but when the flak started to fly Roy promptly hit back at the knockers and his goal at Carrow Road was a telling response.

The football world seemed to be bursting with speculation that we could win all three domestic competitions but even the most enthusiastic of our supporters hesitated when we drew Wimbledon away in the fifth round. Wimbledon at Old Trafford perhaps doesn't frighten us as much as it used to, but who wants to play the Crazy Gang in the Cup away from home? I wasn't particularly looking forward to it myself but perhaps we realised as a team that we had to pull out something special and, in fact, we went to town at Selhurst Park to do the business, 3-0.

We were bang on song right through the side. Eric put us in the driving seat with a great goal just before half-time. One of their defenders cleared a cross from Denis Irwin to the edge of the box. Eric caught it on his right foot, flicked it up in the air and smashed it into the roof of the net. It was a beauty, maybe the goal of the season. We turned it on in the second half with a goal from Incey at a corner and then a nice one to finish with from Denis after a move which involved at least a dozen passes.

Our win did not come easy because we had to stand up for ourselves early in the game. After only two minutes, for instance, Vinnie Jones flattened Roy with a late tackle. The Irishman kept control, however, and our men at the back also stood firm against the power of Fashanu. But, as I was saying earlier, we've got the Wimbledon aggression pretty well taped these days. Gary Pallister and Steve Bruce played well and we were beginning to get, as the gaffer put it, the smell of the Wembley hot-dogs in our nostrils!

The final didn't look so far away when the sixth round gave us Charlton Athletic at home, though it turned out to be quite a traumatic tie for our goalkeeper with a dismissal seconds before the interval whistle. Big Pete steamed out of the penalty area to stop Kim Grant; the ball hit him on the forearm and he also carted his opponent. I don't think the ref, Robbie Hart, had much choice but to point to the dressing-

The prodigal son returns home as Mark Hughes signs on again for Manchester United flanked by manager Alex Ferguson and chairman Martin Edwards

Mark wheels away after giving United a 2-1 lead against Crystal Palace in the 1990 FA Cup final

The victory parade at Wembley after the FA Cup success against Palace which proved a major turning point in the history of the club

Down but far from out as Mark signals his equaliser for a replay against Palace and an eventual 1-0 win

United line up in readiness for the final of the European Cup Winners Cup in Rotterdam

Barcelona kicked and tripped Mark but couldn't stop their old team-mate emerging the two-goal hero of United's European triumph

Sweet revenge as two-goal Hughes brandishes the Cup Winners Cup after a final against the club which labelled him a flop

Mark collects the Player of the Year award in 1991, his second PFA award in three years following his return from Barcelona

Wedding day with Jill, the girl he met back home in Wrexham, and best man Clayton Blackmore, a lifelong friend and team-mate at Old Trafford as well as a fellow Welsh international

A not-so-serious Mark Hughes with Jill at United's Christmas party in 1992

Runners-up in the League to Leeds in 1992 but Mark could still wave a
Rumbelows Cup winners medal after beating Nottingham Forest at Wembley

room. That, needless to say, did not stop the boss from a repeat performance of the Norwich harangue! He announced that the handball was not deliberate and that the club would therefore consider an appeal. He might have had a point but even at the time I wondered how this would excuse Pete kicking his opponent up in the air!

However, back to Charlton. We were down to ten men in the second half but delivered the goods for a 3-1 win. I grabbed a goal as soon as we got back on the field and Andrei stole the show to score twice. His second involved him racing half the length of the pitch and it was from this moment that he really began to hit the kind of form that made the club desperate to sign him on again in the summer. That Ukrainian really has a great turn of speed, and I think it was a tragedy that he and a few fellow Russian internationals got involved in a dispute that kept them out of the World Cup in America this summer.

Andrei was signed as something of an unknown quantity from Donetsk towards the end of season 1990–91. It was obvious he could run fast but equally clear that as far as the manager was concerned he had a bit to learn about the United team plan. He was also unlucky to find himself competing with two such promising wingers as Ryan Giggs and Lee Sharpe. He spent a great deal of our first Championship-winning season on the bench. In fact, he was as often a substitute as he was in the starting line-up and you could see he didn't like it. Indeed, the rumour in the dressing-room was that he intended to leave at the first opportunity. I also felt sorry for him so far away from home with a very young wife who had the tragic experience of losing her first baby. They must have felt very lonely at times, away from their families, but you could see he always tried hard to stay cheerful and I'm delighted to say that they now have a beautiful baby boy who rejoices in the lovely name of Andrei Andreivich (if that's how you spell it!).

I guess most fans considered fate was urging us towards the Double when we were drawn against Oldham in the semi-finals. On paper, it looked the best possible draw for us because the Latics were having a hard time and eventually finished the season as relegation victims. I was sorry for them because while they have been in the top division we have had some tremendously exciting tussles with them. Perhaps I am also influenced by the fact that we have run up some of our biggest scores against our near neighbours! Last season, for instance, we won 5-2 at Boundary Park in the League and just the week before the Cup tie we had put three past them at Old Trafford. At the same time, there was a niggle deep down when I recalled the tremendous semi-final struggle we had had against the Latics in 1990 on our way to winning the FA Cup against Crystal Palace.

We were clear favourites on that occasion at Maine Road but Oldham played out of their skins to frighten us to death with a 3-3 draw to earn a replay. Even in the second game we were taken to extra time in a thrill-a-minute match and it wasn't until very late that substitute Mark Robins got us through 2-1. I was right to have some misgivings this time because we were within a minute of seeing our dreams float through the window at Wembley. The FA had taken the match to London, which I thought was a ridiculous decision for two Northern teams, but that's by the way. Perhaps playing at Wembley lifted the Latics because they again rose to the occasion to take us into extra time with no score at the end of 90 minutes. Eric Cantona was still missing as he served his five-match ban and suspensions also saw us without Roy and Andrei. Even so, we should have been strong enough to have accounted for a team at the bottom of the table. You just can't take the boys from Boundary Park for granted though, and when Neil Pointon put them ahead just after the break in extra time, it looked like curtains for us.

We were all dashing about like headless chickens and I know I had lost my cool because I was booked for having a go at Craig Fleming, who had marked me extremely well throughout the match. I am happy to say that I was able to make amends by getting us out of gaol to earn a replay with less than a minute to go. Brian McClair chipped a great ball over the heads of the Oldham defenders and as it dropped over my shoulder I smashed it into the back of the net for a life-saving goal. I don't think Jon Hallworth saw it and it was a goal I shall treasure for the rest of my life.

Was it a fluke? Some might say that I just instinctively lashed out but I would argue that there was a bit more to it than that. To be honest, I score goals like that because, for a centre-forward, I'm lousy with headers on goal. So, I practise at the training ground with balls knocked to me in mid-air so that I can volley them from all kinds of angles. It's something I've worked hard at. Like many things in sport, the more time you spend in practice, the better you get. Like golf, it's all about timing and, with just a few seconds left to reach Wembley, I have never timed one better! Also at work was a fear of failure. I knew as the ball was coming down that it was probably our last chance. If I had missed, we would have been dead and buried for the FA Cup, the Double would have been a dead duck and we might not even have won the Championship. It would have been extremely difficult to have lifted ourselves after such a big disappointment, so it was a key moment and our big break.

People were very kind about my effort. Joe Royle described it as a flash of genius and added: 'I just couldn't see a goal coming. It was going to take something out of the blue. When the ball dropped, it would have gone over the stand with most players but unfortunately for us it fell to Mark Hughes. You just can't legislate for that kind of strike.'

The boss said: 'When you are a goal down with less than a minute to go, you need a miracle. Thanks to Sparky, that's what we got. Happily, his speciality has so often been to score at important moments.'

The replay was arranged for Maine Road, where it should have been in the first place. Even the FA resisted the idea of taking two sets of Northern supporters down to London twice in a week. Oldham were bitterly disappointed but they put a brave face on it, with their manager reminding everyone that Maine Road was a good ground for them. They were bidding for their first ever appearance in an FA Cup final but, ironically, one of their old boys, Denis Irwin, went through and with the help of Bryan Robson, scored after only ten minutes to make it difficult for them. Then when Andrei, who always seems to play well against the Latics, put us further ahead just five minutes later after an amazing run, they were really up against it. Typically, they launched a fight-back and pulled a goal back through Neil Pointon just before the break. That was the signal for Robbo to get busy and in the second half he steamed in at a corner to force home the ball for what Joe Royle later described as 'a killer'.

It was almost as important as my goal in the first game, for it knocked the stuffing out of the Latics. Andrei and Ryan cut loose on the flanks and Ryan made it 4-1, to leave poor old Joe lamenting again the cruelty and injustice of my late equaliser. You can't afford sentiment in sport when it comes to the business of winning and losing, though, and our immediate concern was that we had given our fans their fifth Wembley final in four years, not a bad achievement. And with Wembley now put on a back-burner it meant we could concentrate all our efforts on one last big push for the Championship.

The match must have prompted mixed feelings for Bryan Robson. On the one hand, he had come back to demonstrate that there was plenty of life still left in the old dog but it was also the occasion when he formally stood down as our captain after leading the team through thick and thin since taking over from Ray Wilkins back in his early days under Ron Atkinson.

For some time he had been acting in tandem with Steve Bruce, wearing the armband when he was playing but leaving Steve to do the job when he wasn't there. At the presentation of the Championship trophy the previous season they had both gone up together and shared the honour. But when we went out for the replay at Maine Road Robbo returned to the ranks and Brucey was the skipper. The boss told us that it made more sense for Steve to stay as captain and he said Bryan was satisfied these days just to win a place in the team. At the same time, it must have brought home to him that his days at Old Trafford were finally running out and that even Captain Fantastic, at the age of 37, couldn't carry on forever!

Meanwhile, we wrapped up the title and then set out for London to face Chelsea, hoping to avoid the kind of ill luck which robbed Manchester United of a League and FA Cup double in 1957. That was the year just before the Munich tragedy, when United, the League champions, met Aston Villa in the Cup final only to have their goalkeeper, Ray Wood, carried off with a smashed cheekbone. There were no substitutes in those days and Villa beat the ten men.

We weren't anticipating that kind of problem, of course. Our biggest worry was the fact that Chelsea had beaten us twice in the League and clearly had a bit of an Indian sign on us, with that man Gavin Peacock clearly a problem. Still, we were back to full strength. Big Peter, who had missed the final two League games after aggravating an ankle injury at Ipswich that he had been carrying for some time, declared himself fit and all the other players who had been rested for the Coventry match had got over their bumps and bruises. I was one of the players left out because of my heel injury, but I was up and ready for Wembley.

The boss kept our preparations as normal as possible. We didn't travel down to London until the Thursday. Brian McClair and Lee Sharpe were the unlucky players who found themselves on the substitutes' bench, with Bryan Robson bitterly disappointed to find himself not even in the playing squad. By then his talks with Middlesbrough were quite advanced so he had something to soften the blow. Chelsea were the underdogs, but you wouldn't have thought it in the early stages. They were very chipper and there was no score by half-time. Indeed, Peacock had hit the bar to remind us that he knows the way to our goal. The turning point came, ironically enough, from the penalty spot. I say ironically because we had only been awarded two penalties in the whole of the season before the final. So it was quite unexpected to find referee David Elleray awarding us two in the space of five minutes!

First Eddie Newton tripped Denis Irwin as our full-back made a run into the box and then Frank Sinclair brought Andrei down. The awards were like a gift from heaven, but they still had to be scored. Fortunately for us, we have just the man: Joe Cool himself. The French are supposed to be an excitable race but, though he does have his temperamental moments, Eric is brilliant under this kind of pressure.

Dennis Wise came up with some gamesmanship for the first and tried to put Eric off by offering a £100 bet that he would miss. A complaint was also made that he hadn't put the ball properly on the penalty spot as he stroked his shot past Dmitri Kharine. He shrugged off all the distractions and did exactly the same again five minutes later to put us two goals up and just about break the hearts of the Londoners. Steve Bruce served us well when he was our penalty-taker but he would be the first to concede that Eric is a master. The justice of the second penalty I'm not absolutely sure about. Chelsea certainly complained that it was six of one and half a dozen of the other as Andrei raced alongside Sinclair. That's the way it goes, though, and we certainly weren't complaining. Indeed, we were jolly relieved because until we had gone in front we weren't playing particularly well.

Once in front it was plain sailing. I slotted in a goal and

an unselfish Paul Ince put one on a plate for Brian McClair who had come on as a substitute, to give us an impressive-looking scoreline of 4-0. I must say, we were flattered, but no one was thinking along those lines as we hailed the first League and FA Cup double in our long history. It's an achievement that eluded even the legendary Sir Matt and it was fitting that we finally managed it in the season which saw him pass away. We all felt it was a most appropriate and timely tribute to the great man.

The big and elusive dream had become reality and we all know we have written a rare chapter into the history of the club. I am proud of my contribution as my Cup final score brought me to a total of 22 goals, my best since playing along-side Frank Stapleton before I went abroad. It was also satisfying to know that I had scored the team's first goal of the season when we had played in the Charity Shield at Wembley and then I had signed off by scoring in our final game in front of the Twin Towers!

It was a good match for my partner, too. His goals brought his season's tally to 25 and he had more than won back his spurs after the outbursts which cost him his five-fixture suspension. Eric rooms with Peter Schmeichel and the Dane knows him as well as anyone off the field as well as on it. To say that Pete is his number-one fan is putting it mildly, but I think we would all agree with his post-match summing up, when he said: 'When I saw Eric put the ball on the penalty spot I knew the Double was safe. I have faced him a lot in training and he is a very hard player to read because he reads you. He is just marvellous, incredible. I have never played with or against anybody like him and I have played against most of the game's top players. What he has done for our team is fantastic. In football terms he is not of this world, he is from another planet.

'He might go missing for ten minutes in a game but he can win everything for you in a second. Eric was made for

United and United were made for Eric Cantona. Whenever the ball drops for him in the opposing box I just get ready for another kick-off. I just know he will score, that's the degree of confidence I have in him. Now that's good!

'Everybody keeps asking if he will stay at Old Trafford, and he is, of course, a bit of a wandering star but I think he will. The way he plays, the way he acts, has United written all over him. I cannot see him going anywhere else. Not when he enjoys the football, enjoys the life and enjoys the club the way he does. He's a good guy, nothing like his media image or the reputation some have given him. Eric is more an angel then a devil.'

Eric is halfway through a four-year contract and I don't think he will walk out on it, which, as his partner, suits me down to the ground. We have got something special going and you couldn't mistake his joy as we celebrated our Wembley victory and the Double.

I'll never forget him saying: 'The best trophy to win is always the last one you lifted and every time you succeed at something you must then try to get even better, and that means you must try to win everything. This is the best team I have ever played in, and we not only win things, we play with pleasure.'

He has a philosophical turn of phrase, does Eric, and half the time I wonder whether he tries to wind up his interviewers, but he is entitled to spout on about the game a bit because he is the best.

I'm not so sure the Chelsea supporters thought the referee was the best. Most of those I spoke to accepted that the first penalty given by David Elleray was fair enough, and, let's face it, they couldn't dispute it the way Denis went cartwheeling into the air. They were furious about the Kanchelskis award, though, because they thought Frank Sinclair had done nothing but run alongside our man in a fair challenge for the ball. So I was interested in the comments of this public-school master in charge of the game. He said his conscience was clear and went on: 'I can understand Chelsea's disappointment but at no time did the defender try to play the ball. I had refereed both teams several times in the season and the players were aware of the standards I accept.'

Eric, by the way, became the first player to score two penalties in an FA Cup final played at Wembley, an event with a history of over 70 years. It is just one more achievement for a player they used to call the bad boy of football.

What made our season unique in my opinion was that alongside achieving the Double we reached the final of the Coca-Cola Cup. Admittedly, we didn't last long in Europe but even so it added up to playing a total of 63 competitive matches and for long periods we were regularly playing twice a week, especially when you take into account the fact that most of our team were involved in international football.

The League Cup competition, played under a variety of different sponsors' names over the years, is fast becoming an embarrassment for the top clubs involved in the European competitions, especially now that the European Cup is being played after the preliminary rounds on a league basis which involves a minimum of six games. I just don't know how a club which progresses in the Coca-Cola Cup is going to handle the inevitable clash of fixtures.

I see that the Premier League appreciate the possible problems and have notified the Football League, who run the League Cup, that they have told their clubs that they can pick from their squad. This is a variation on the old rule that you must always field your strongest team. The change means you could in effect play your reserve side because, under the current system of squad numbering, some players wear numbers as high as 30 or over! I have read that our manager intends to play some of the youngsters and, of course, the senior fringe players in the Coca-Cola Cup, and under the present arrangements I don't see any alternative.

The answer, I believe, is to shift the whole competition

to the first half of the season so that it is complete by Christmas. I am not knocking the competition, because I appreciate that it is an opportunity for smaller clubs to raise revenue, and even for the major sides it carries the attraction of qualifying the winners to play in the UEFA Cup. It's just that under the present format it is an embarrassment for successful clubs and likely to become even more so this season. I think there will have to be change or before long there is going to be an almighty snarl-up.

Our boss approached it with obvious mixed feelings last season and right from day one said he was going to use it to benefit the players not getting regular League football. I am sure players like Brian McClair, Bryan Robson, Dion Dublin, Mike Phelan and Lee Martin welcomed it. They were all in the team which played at Stoke in the first leg of our opening round, though we probably fell between two stools as we came a cropper with a 2-1 defeat. It wasn't the regular reserve side but it wasn't our usual first team either, and there were so many changes we just didn't get going properly.

It was also probably in the back of our minds that we had a second leg at Old Trafford to come and, indeed, we polished them off quite well on our own ground. The boss still left Eric and Paul Ince out but there were fewer changes. Dion had scored us a valuable goal at the Victoria Ground so that when Brian McClair and Lee Sharpe came up with the goods we were through. Perhaps only four changes from our usual line-up, as opposed to seven for the first leg, made the difference.

We didn't mess about in the next round, beating Leicester City 5-1 at Old Trafford. There were still changes in the side, but we clicked so impressively that Colin Gibson, our old left-back who moved on after a bad knee injury, delivered the verdict that he would happily pay to watch us. 'Such quality and so many crosses from the wingers,' he enthused. I imagine Leicester's morale must have sagged when they saw Lee Sharpe taken off after a telling display only to see Ryan Giggs take his place! Steve Bruce stole the scoring show, heading in the first and last goals. In between, Brian McClair, Lee Sharpe and I helped ourselves to goals in a morale-boosting win. Brucey summed himself up well when he said: 'I'm just a frustrated striker at heart.'

The Coca-Cola went on ice for nearly three months and when we resumed at home to Portsmouth we got something of a shock. Paul Walsh called on the experience gathered during his extensive travels to grab a couple of goals with the help of a little uncertainty at the back, and they fought all the way to deserve their 2-2 draw. A replay was the last thing we needed at that busy stage of the season in January and not everyone fancied our chances down at Fratton Park. I was left out to rest my heel injury, but otherwise the boss had returned to playing a full-strength team. By then, just two games short of Wembley and to ensure a European place, he clearly wanted to win it.

Brian, who had taken my place, duly obliged by scoring to give us a 1-0 win. It was his fourth goal of the season, which considering he had made only 11 starts was a good return. It was a difficult night with a stiff wind and bumpy pitch but we showed we were capable of grinding out a winning result without being spectacular. We were now enjoying one of our best spells of the season, so that even though Sheffield Wednesday presented an obvious challenge in the semi-final we all felt confident, particularly with the semi-finals of this competition played over two legs.

Wednesday came to Old Trafford for the first leg with the idea of stopping us playing, but their plan came unstuck when Ryan caught a defender in possession, robbed him, and then streaked away to go round Kevin Pressman and score a beauty from the narrowest of angles. They had to come out on the attack more after that, but David Hirst and Chris Waddle, their main attacking strengths, were only just back from long injury lay-offs and it showed.

Hillsborough is not a place which scares us any more and, thanks to early goals from Choccy McClair and Andrei, we were soon well on top in the second leg. Hirst gave them some hope with a goal but I scored twice in as comfortable a semi-final win as I can recall. We had, in fact, played so well in that match and in the other competitions around that time – we had just polished off Wimbledon 3-0 in the FA Cup – that talk of us doing a magic treble reached fever pitch.

By the time the Coca-Cola Cup final came around towards the end of March our form had dipped slightly, though we were still odds-on to lay the foundations for a treble-trophy season. Aston Villa had other ideas for Wembley, though, and in our old manager, Ron Atkinson, they had a man who knows the psychology and make-up of our club almost as well as Alex Ferguson. Anyway, he came up with a plan to stop us playing while banking on giving us a sucker-punch to win and it worked a treat for them.

We were without Big Pete in goal but you couldn't blame defeat on Les Sealey. They had five men in midfield and they caught us cold after 26 minutes, when Dean Saunders flicked a ball forward for Dalian Atkinson to race through and give Villa the lead. Eric was making his first appearance after being sent off in successive matches. With the prospect of impending suspension hanging over him, it was hardly surprising that he couldn't work any magic for us. I thought we stuck at it but quarter of an hour from the end Saunders stuck out a foot to deflect a free kick past Les and they were really in the driving-seat. I got a goal back but there were only seven minutes left. I thought I had beaten Mark Bosnich again to force extra time with a strong shot but he made a good stop and sent his team up the other end for a last-minute penalty.

This was Andrei's unlucky moment when he stopped a shot from Atkinson with his arm. He was sent off and Saunders made it 3-1 with a spot-kick. It was our lowest point of the season, what with all the sendings-off and a run of drawn matches to bring Blackburn into the title race. I didn't like the Wembley pitch, with the grass too long and lush holding up the pace of our speedy wingers, but we couldn't really complain. The boss reckoned we had worked hard but it was left to Dean Saunders to put into words what everyone was thinking. He wanted to know if the defeat would burst the Old Trafford bubble, and as he added, it was the biggest disappointment we had had for a long time.

Would we go to pieces or would the reverse strengthen our resolve to go on and win an FA Cup and League double? We know the answer now, of course, and I think it speaks volumes for the spirit and make-up of Manchester United that that is exactly what we proceeded to do.

Chapter Five

OR WHINGERS?

SO what exactly is the character of Manchester United these days: are we an argumentative and unruly bunch, as some were claiming at one point in the season, or is it that we are just such a high-profile club that everything we do is magnified beyond normal reason?

As I mentioned earlier, we were accused of being paranoid and over-sensitive to criticism when we came under fire after a succession of dismissals on the last lap for the Double. We were analysed in all sections of the media and we took quite a lot of flak. We were told by one tabloid paper that we were moaners, groaners and whingers. They hit us particularly hard after the Swindon game, when Eric Cantona was sent off for the infamous stamping incident. Words like disgrace and thuggery were flying around as if we were devils incarnate.

We were told: 'Roy Keane, a huge talent, wants to fight the world every time he is tackled, judged offside or disagrees with the referee. Denis Irwin complained so much to the linesman he was lucky not to be sent off. Paul Ince is a moaner. Mark Hughes is a fireball waiting to explode. Touch him and he turns on you like a street fighter.'

But the real vitriol was reserved for our Frenchman. The reporter went on: 'Cantona was a disgrace to himself, the great name of Manchester United and more importantly to English football. He is a genius but he cannot stand being out-played. He proved himself a coward. I hope the FA charge him with bringing the game into disrepute and ban him for ten games. This is what he deserves for his vicious stamp into the chest of Swindon's John Moncur.

'It has been coming all season. He should have been sent off at Norwich for backheeling John Polston but, unlike Leicestershire referee Brian Hill, Portland official Paul Durkin bottled it,' he concluded.

Lawrie Sanchez, the Swindon forward who used to play for Wimbledon, which might explain a great deal, was recruited to have a go at us as well. He was reported as saying: 'If Cantona played for Wimbledon he would be sent off every week. He has been doing it all season. We've all seen it on TV and Brian Hill was brave enough to send him off. I am sure Alex Ferguson will complain and say Cantona was unfairly treated but to the rest of us it was no contest. He had to go. You can't be allowed to trample on players and get away with it. United and Cantona have been getting away with murder all season. Like the Liverpool of old, they get protected. Prima donnas don't believe they should be tackled or challenged. We rattled them, we outplayed and outfought them and they didn't like it. Ferguson should have been big enough to condemn Cantona.'

Well, they certainly slammed us all right, and though I wouldn't claim that we were all angels I think the press reaction was ridiculously exaggerated and over the top. Manchester United sells newspapers and the competition is such these days that they are desperate for big stories about us.

Everything is made out to be larger than life, even the things we do well and our successes, but, boy, do they go to town when we step out of line.

We got a real taste of it, too, when we went to Turkey for the second leg of our European Cup tie against Galatasaray. All right, Eric went overboard and lost his head, but the intimidation and provocation was unbelievable. I didn't play in that match in Istanbul because of the foreigner rule and I sat in the stand with other players not directly involved. We were wearing our United tracksuits and I can tell you we sat tight until the crowd had cleared. The hostility was unbelievable and I doubt if we would have got to the dressing-rooms in one piece if we had attempted it at the final whistle.

It's in this kind of volatile atmosphere that you must judge emotional players such as Eric Cantona. I am not saying he was blameless – and he knows he was out of line – but I think the media savaged him. By the time I got to the dressing-room, Eric was fuming and apparently all hell had been let loose. Our players had had to run a gauntlet of hate and it seemed as if the police, who were meant to protect them, had been just as biased. Robbo had split his arm after being hit by one of the police shields and everyone had been jostled on the way to the safety of the dressing-room. Eric, of course, had clashed with the referee at the end of the game and had been booked – a rash moment which now sees him banned from our first four European Cup games this season.

The big man just loves his football and it's that great desire to play the game the right way that, from time to time, lands him in trouble. There is a common theme that runs through all the matches which have seen him in bother, be it at Norwich, Swindon, Arsenal or Galatasaray. In his view, players have not behaved and he's got riled. The fundamental reason has been his frustration. He gets annoyed if he is not allowed to play the game the way he believes it should be played, especially if opponents are cheating and illegal methods are being employed to stop him that aren't dealt with properly by the referee.

The other factor is that his name goes before him. Give a dog a bad name in football and it sticks, particularly if you come with the kind of lurid reputation Eric brought with him from France after becoming too hot to handle. If you ask me, he has got his temper much more under control. He still faces a lot of provocation out on the park and rivals try to wind him up. Occasionally, they succeed but I believe he has done remarkably well to keep his head as well as he has.

In a way, I suppose I am very like Eric – a fireball waiting to explode, as I was described, or an accident waiting to happen – but I consider this aspect of my character vastly over-played. I accept that I feel the need to be physically involved in a tough match, otherwise I don't experience any sense of fulfilment. If I took the in-built aggression and competitive edge out of my natural game I wouldn't be half the player. But I will stress one simple fact: nobody ever gets seriously hurt playing against me. I believe defenders respect me for that. They know they are not going to get crippled high across the knees or have an elbow smashed into their faces that leaves them with a busted nose. They might finish up with a few bumps and bruises because I'll certainly knock my markers over. I'll even rough them up a bit – in the same way that they do to let me know they're about – but nothing more.

I am very combative out on the park. It's a hard and uncompromising game if you are going to be a winner but I see nothing wrong in that. If somebody is trying to stop me reaching for the prizes then I will compete to the limit. There is a limit, though, and I won't cross the line to land in the kind of situation that has been figuring in recent court cases. As I say, when I knock defenders down, they get up again. My conscience is clear about the way I do the business. I don't think there is an opponent who can honestly say he has reason to hold a grudge against me. If they say I'm a handful, that's fair enough and I take it as a compliment. All this talk about Sparky the mean hatchet-man, the footballer who goes to war, is stretching things too far. I am not going to change my footballing character now, either. With a growing maturity, I believe I am a better player than I was in my younger days. Off the field, I think everyone will tell you that I wouldn't say boo to a goose. It would probably take a punch on the hooter to get me to react physically. I accept my character changes once I get on to the park. In fact, there is nothing I enjoy more than a good, hard, rough game, especially if the crowd is hostile and really having a go.

Some players are intimidated by the crowd but unless it reaches Galatasaray proportions, I am lifted when there are thousands screaming at me. It inspires me when I savour the situation as I know that I can make them even more angry because I am out there on the pitch and there is nothing they can do to stop me. I can't explain why I am such a different person once the whistle has gone. It's just the way I am. It's the crowd, the atmosphere and the emotion. I may not be one of the most liked players on opposing grounds but that's no problem for me. I'll always be aggressive. My game is taking the rough stuff and all the knocks. I don't mind taking the pressure off Eric because that's not really his type of game. I'm prepared to get stuck in and let him get on with the kind of stylish football he's better at than me. Mind you, as we have seen, from time to time Eric doesn't duck away or hide either. He's a big man and he's capable of dishing it out. Lawrie Sanchez must be crazy to call him a coward – perhaps he has figured that, playing for Swindon, he is unlikely to come face to face with him in the future.

I believe the present United team, while reaching new standards of skill, technique and vision, is also a much stronger team physically. Sometimes in the past I have felt that, with notable exceptions, we weren't a particularly hard side and that other teams exploited our weakness. It's not a problem now. You need a balance and I reckon the manager has achieved it with the players he has assembled. Our results last season were the reward.

I'm certainly not going to change, because it would make me a lesser player and with everyone itching to knock us off our pedestal it is important we make it clear that we are not going to be bullied or frightened out of it. Even more important, we are going to try harder to resist attempts to wind us up into any more red-card situations. Eric and I are probably the prime targets if an opponent fancies trying to make us see red. As we have shown a few times, we have our explosive side and there have been moments we have deeply regretted.

I was sent off at Sheffield United and I wish it hadn't happened. I was wrong to kick Tuttle and no one can condone that kind of behaviour. I am sure I speak for Eric as well when I say that we would dearly love to eliminate rash retaliation and wild moments. We have to be strong enough to look after ourselves without reacting when opponents try to kick us or wind us up. We are working very hard on getting on with the game, no matter what the provocation.

It's easy to snap but we learned a lesson last season. There is too much at stake, and the consequences too serious, to start looking for retribution or getting on to the wrong side of the law. I don't wish to tempt fate and make out that we are completely reformed characters who will now be able to lead blameless footballing lives, because, as I have explained, we walk a knife's edge with our particular personalities.

Nevertheless, we shall try and I am always much encouraged when I read reports of opponents testifying that I am not a butcher – and there have been a few, I'll have you know, who can share a ding-dong while still retaining a respect for each other. For instance, I came across a cutting the other day which quoted Southampton's granite centre-half Kevin Moore saying: 'Mark is as good a leader of the front line as you will find in this country and has a great physical presence.

He likes a dust-up on the pitch and you come out of a match with him feeling tender but there is nothing illegal about his style. At the end of our match against United last week he offered me his hand and I was happy to shake it.'

Yes, that's how I like it, and there are plenty of defenders I am happy to have a drink with later after the cut-and-thrust of a hard game. The last centre-half to put me on my back and knock the wind out of me was Neil Ruddock when we played Liverpool at Old Trafford. Actually, I couldn't find him for the rest of the game. I kept telling the lads to put a high one up over his head but I think he had retreated to sweeper! Anyway, Neil, rough and tough with Southampton and Spurs, is OK and there will be no hard feelings when we meet again this season.

Paul McGrath I rate the best in the business but he is so good that he doesn't need to get involved in a trial of strength. I never thought, though, that I would find myself with a rival central defender living virtually next door, and one from the deadly Manchester City camp at that, but sure enough Keith Curle is my neighbour. I wondered for a while how a tough derby and perhaps an explosive ding-dong with my marker would do for a quiet home life. Fortunately, Keith tends to play more as a sweeper and we are not often face to face so war has not yet been declared in the Cheshire rural peace of Mottram!

Of course, controversy about my way of playing is nothing new. Three years ago Louis Nicollin, the President of Montpellier, called me a cheat and I was accused of deliberately taking a dive in an attempt to get one of their players, Pascal Baills, sent off. The incident happened in the first leg of our European Cup Winners Cup quarter-final against the French team at Old Trafford. They said I pretended to be head-butted by Baills so that the referee would have no option but to dismiss him, incurring an automatic suspension for the second leg. Their President actually said I shouldn't go to

France, which was a very threatening and inflammatory remark.

I was disgusted by the allegation. All I knew at the time was that someone had run at me like an express train and knocked me down. It wasn't a matter of pretending: the guy had knocked the wind out of me and if I held my head it was because he had caught me on the side of the face with his shoulder. He hadn't head-butted me and I didn't try to make it look as if he had. Looking back on it, I think the Montpellier players knew their man was in trouble with the referee so they immediately tried to suggest I was play-acting to try and get him off the hook. It just goes to show – like our experience in Istanbul – that playing in European competition is a whole new ball game and that you have to be prepared for a whole new range of trickery.

Mind you, I doubt whether anything could have been more bizarre than our ill-fated trip to Turkey, as I am sure the United supporters who made the journey would testify. Many of them had a nightmare experience in the face of appalling treatment from the Turkish authorities. The people I felt sorriest for were those who were roused from their beds in the middle of the night before the game. The police told them they were being taken to another hotel for their own safety. Who would argue with that in the small hours of the morning or say they would prefer to stay and take the risk? So they all packed and got on to buses, only to find themselves being taken to police stations and locked up for the rest of the night.

The conditions were primitive, from what I have been told, and it wasn't a very pleasant experience. Elderly folk and women, it didn't make any difference, they were all moved. Some of them hardly ate and they spent their time in cells until they were finally told they would be escorted to the match. So on the buses they went again, only to find another dirty trick being pulled on them. They weren't taken to the ground, they were driven instead to the airport and put on the plane home with their passports stamped 'deported', a very serious situation for anyone wanting to travel abroad in the future, be it on holiday, business or even another football trip, if they could find the courage and interest after such diabolical treatment.

Some fans from other hotels who missed the dragnet and duly went to the ground couldn't get in because the police said it was full and they were too late. It really was disgraceful and, as you might expect, the Football Supporters Association and a number of MPs channelled complaints to the Government. I believe the Home Office came up with an offer of new passports without the telling 'deported' stamp, though whether these had to be paid for I'm not sure. There was talk of asking for compensation, especially refunds on the tickets which they were unable to use. I think United have tried to put pressure on Galatasaray through UEFA but so far without much success.

The best I heard was an offer from the Turkish Government this summer of five free holidays to United supporters as a goodwill gesture. One lady's reaction was: 'Turkey can get stuffed!' And now we have to play there again this season. The Turks beat Avenir Beggen 5-1 in the first leg of their preliminary round in Luxembourg, 4–0 at home and so play in our group. I bet Eric is almost glad he is suspended for the first leg in Istanbul.

But Istanbul is not the only hell I have come across. Everything seems rosy now, what with the plaudits for our Wembley victory and Championship successes still ringing in my ears, my medals and caps all safely stored to show my kids, a lovely wife and home, money in the bank and the fans chanting 'Hughesie'. It hasn't always been like that and at the beginning I had to fight my corner like everyone else. More than once my football future was on the line.

I was reminded of my modest beginnings only last May when Lou Macari brought Glasgow Celtic down for my testimonial and said he remembered me as a youngster when he was a senior player at Old Trafford. He pointed out that I deserved credit for what I had achieved because it was obvious, so he claimed, that in my early days I wasn't blessed with as much talent as other players. It was a back-handed compliment and it reminded me that life certainly wasn't all plain sailing when I reported to Old Trafford as a fresh-faced schoolboy from my little village of Ruabon a few miles from Wrexham.

Ron Atkinson was the manager as I worked my way through the junior sides and he didn't seem in any rush at all to give me a chance in the first team. I had played regularly in the youth side but Norman Whiteside was his favourite among us junior reserves. Brian Whitehouse, the reserve-team coach, kept plugging me but big Ron didn't seem to rate me. He kept passing me over and his favourite pastime seemed to be teasing me.

Perhaps it was his way of trying to get me to improve my application and attitude. Quite a few times he had me in his office to spell out that unless I pushed myself a bit harder my career was going nowhere except out of the door. I suppose I was about 17, shy and homesick and finding the hurly-burly of a football club hard to take on board.

At every opportunity I was off back home to my village and a set of pals I had grown up with. I found I was able to relax better, forget my problems and the worries of whether I was going to make the grade or not. I suppose it was an escape. I was proud of myself for sticking with my old mates. I didn't want them to think that because I was with a big soccer club I had become too high and mighty for them. As a teenager, I would have been mortified by that thought.

I have never been built for speed and I made all kinds of excuses about carrying a knock or having a bit of a cold. Really, though, I should have been taken on one side and straightened out.

I lived with the same landlady from the age of 16 just a couple of houses down from the Cliff training ground. It was very convenient because if necessary I could get from my bed to the dressing-room in a matter of seconds. I was well looked after and I made a big mistake after I had had a pay rise. I thought, in my immature wisdom, that I was a big boy and should be getting a place of my own, so I took a flat in Bowdon. It was very nice but I found Cheshire a bit different from Salford in those days. I had been used to a few mates dropping in to my digs because I was so handy, but when I had my posh flat I was so far away from anyone nobody came. I was even more home-sick – a taste of what it was going to be like in Barcelona!

My last season at United before my transfer was particularly upsetting because midway through I was persuaded to sign the secret deal which took me to Barcelona. I was sworn to secrecy because the Spanish club didn't want to unsettle their other foreign players and United didn't want to upset our fans. Rumours started inevitably to fly and I had to lie. I wasn't at all comfortable with that and I found it difficult to handle. The whole situation was aggravated by a sudden slump in not just my form but that of the whole team. We had made that brilliant start to season 1985–86, when I told you we had played some of the best football I had ever experienced as we put together a run of 15 League games before losing our first match of the season.

It was only my second full season in the senior side. After an injury in the first team, I was given my first ever start with the big boys in the League Cup against Oxford in November 1983. I got the goal in a 1–1 draw for a replay, though it didn't do me much good because I was promptly dropped – that's how much Ron thought of me. I didn't make my full League début for another four months, but happily I scored on that occasion, too, so things began to look up. I got in for the last six League games of the season and all told in seven League appearances scored four goals.

That booked me a regular place for the following season, which is when I first made a few people sit up and take notice. I scored 16 League goals in a season's total of 25 in all competitions. That made Terry Venables at Barcelona look as well so that when we made our blistering start to the following season he launched into a confidential deal with Ron Atkinson and Martin Edwards for my transfer to Spain. That's when I started to fret and fume all over again because at the bottom of my heart I didn't want to go.

The money was fine, and let's not beat about the bush, I went for the cash. I was still young and immature, though, and I wasn't ready to make such a big break. The idea of leaving was torture. On the one hand, my advisers insisted that this was an opportunity I just could not turn down. They argued that it might not happen again and that in football you have got to strike while the iron is hot. I could understand all that. I could hear what they were saying, but when I was on my own I just wanted to stay in my local scene and do well for Manchester United, who at that stage were promising to take the game by storm and I was very much part of it.

On top of all that, my romance had recently begun with Jill, now my wife of course, after meeting her in Wrexham's one and only nightclub, and I had a lot of thinking and talking to do with her about our future commitment. Obviously, if I was going away we had to decide one way or the other what was going to happen to us as an item. So it was all very unsettling. I was very flattered, of course. I had hardly been in the game five minutes and here I was on the receiving end of a financially very attractive offer. The situation on that side of things was that for a player currently knocking in a lot of goals I was on relatively modest money at United, certainly a lot less than most of my team-mates. Because I had come through the ranks and hadn't looked all that impressive anyway. I was on £200 a week.

Fair enough, the club realised that I was being underpaid

and started to negotiate, which complicated the situation more than ever. I had about 18 months remaining and because I was very naïve in those days I kept putting off an agreement. I think United interpreted this as a ploy on my part to run out of contract so that I would be a free agent and could disappear to Barcelona for only a nominal fee. I'm afraid I wasn't worldly wise enough to have figured that sort of move out and eventually they persuaded me to sign so that I was a player under contract for whom they could ask the £1.8m fee which they were able to extract from Barcelona instead of perhaps less than half that amount.

To me it seemed as if they were pushing me towards the door and in my own mind I got very uptight. The fact that the deal incorporated an option which allowed me to leave five months before the end of the season just made things worse as far as I was concerned. United wanted a breathing space so that they could use me for the rest of the season while Ron Atkinson set about getting a replacement.

I am afraid I was just not the sort of player capable of handling that kind of pressure. Maybe I am now, but as a young man I was still racked by uncertainties about playing on the Continent. What made things worse was that as we entered the second half of the season our form began to dip and guess who was the obvious whipping-boy. A striker whose goals dry up is the soft option for criticism in that kind of situation. Not everyone looks a bit deeper and questions whether it's the service to the men up front which has gone off the boil. I will accept my share of responsibility and I was definitely not a happy man in the second half of that season but there were a few other players who had started to wobble.

The reason for our title fade-out was a collective failure which stemmed from a massive injury list. In a few short but critical weeks, we lost Bryan Robson, Gordon Strachan, Norman Whiteside and Remi Moses. Without them, we lost our rhythm and couldn't maintain the winning tempo. Even when the casualties came back, something had gone and we just weren't the same side.

Before Christmas, thanks to our winning run, we had been ten points clear at the top of the table. Slowly but surely, from December onwards, we lost our grip to finish in fourth place. It wasn't all doom and gloom around that time though, because the previous season we had won the FA Cup. We had some terrific battles to dispose of Bournemouth, Coventry, Blackburn and West Ham before a big one against Liverpool in the semi-finals. I had managed to find the odd goal to help us through to meet Liverpool at Goodison Park and we drew 2-2 after extra time with goals from Bryan Robson and Frank Stapleton. Robbo and myself got the goals for a 2-1 win in the replay at Maine Road. You may recall we beat Everton in the 1985 final with a fantastic strike from my old youth-team buddie, Norman Whiteside.

It took some of the bitterness away from the slide in the League. My scoring form had become erratic but I still managed to score 17 League goals and play in nearly every game. Overall, though finishing fourth in the League is hardly a disgrace, we could not forget the contrast between the way we had started out and the relative collapse at the end. The fans pointed the finger at me as the news of my impending departure began to trickle out into the newspapers. You can't keep that kind of secret in football for very long. The papers had a ready-made scapegoat. They implied that I didn't care any more and that my priority was now the fortune beckoning me to Barcelona. They little knew that I didn't even want to leave a sinking ship!

The criticism hurt because, in my mind I gave everything I had, right to the bitter end. I found it a traumatic time as the day of reckoning drew nearer. I do honestly believe that if Manchester United had made it clear to me that I was part of their plans for the future and had underlined the point by offering me the kind of top money enjoyed by the stars then I don't think I would have gone to Barcelona.

The whole situation was unreal and best summed up by the actual signing ceremony. Around Christmas I was given a day off training in secret in order to fly to Switzerland to meet a Barcelona representative. First I had to fly to London to meet my agent, Dennis Roach, and as a relatively raw kid I got to Manchester Airport without my passport. I drove back to my digs like a fury on a snowy road, skidded and sideswiped the car on the motorway after losing control on a bend. What a way to start the day! I made it in time by the skin of my teeth and eventually met the Barcelona vice-president, Juan Gaspart, in Geneva. I thought I was signing a pre-contract which wouldn't be binding, but it turned out it was. I must have looked as miserable as sin because Señor Gaspart told Dennis I should be the happiest man alive and wanted to know why I wasn't. To celebrate, he took us to a posh restaurant, which required diners to wear jackets. Naturally I hadn't worn one and so I sat through the meal wearing my big leather overcoat. I must have looked as daft as I felt. I tell you the transfer was doomed from the start!

Perhaps my nature makes it difficult for people to get inside my head but I never really wanted to leave Manchester United. I prayed that Barcelona would decide against taking up their transfer option. I hoped something would crop up to change the situation. Even on the day in July when I drove to Manchester airport with my baggage, and Jill to see me off, there was this sinking feeling inside me and nothing seemed real. Of course, it was too late to say anything then. So I kept my mouth shut and it was like being in a dream world. Little did I know that it would turn out to be more a nightmare than a dream!

I'm sure that if I had been married by then, with Jill along to ease the strain, that I would have looked forward to what was undoubtedly a big adventure with a little more relish. Unfortunately, our relationship wasn't far enough down the line at that point for her to uproot herself and come to Spain with me. In fact, she had an uncomfortable and unhappy time back in Wales and the concern about my personal life had not made my position any easier.

I wasn't the only guy having a rough ride that season. It wasn't exactly all plain sailing for Ron Atkinson. Our manager, a flamboyant, larger-than-life character, never really fancied me as a top player. He couldn't have done or he would have done something more to try and keep me at Old Trafford. Perhaps because I was one of the younger players, I was never part of his inner circle. I respected his football philosophy, though. He loved style and players who could play with a touch of magic. He was never the champagne-swigging high-roller that his image suggested to some. He had a tremendous knowledge of the game and the people in it and he was just as much at home with a pot of tea, or rosy lee as he used to call it, as a glass of bubbly. He had a remarkably good record at Old Trafford for a man who was sacked. He always had United finishing in the top four in the League; he won two FA Cup finals and fought a close final with Liverpool in the Milk Cup. He had only one more full season, though, in the Old Trafford hot-seat after I had left. My departure signalled the first rumble because the players he brought in to replace me didn't have the success he hoped for. He bought Peter Davenport, Terry Gibson and, later, Alan Brazil, but although they all had their moments and they again finished fourth the next season, there was something missing from our challenge for the Championship.

Perhaps that's harsh criticism and you have got to remember that Liverpool were enjoying their heyday and were a tough obstacle to shift. I can't honestly say things would have worked out differently had I stayed but it's something I often wonder about.

Chapter Six

Nightmare

MY worst fears were realised just two hours after touchdown in Spain as I landed to prepare for the start of season 1986–87 with Barcelona and I asked myself a question that was to haunt me through 18 miserable months at the Nou Camp: what on earth am I doing here?

Many a time I thought of doing a runner, packing my bags and returning home to my beloved Manchester United and all my friends. Pride, a professional acceptance of my situation and the fact that I was taking the money so I must stay with it stopped me, but it didn't stop me secretly eating my heart out.

I hate to sound petty in the face of a lucrative contract which almost overnight had translated me from a run-of-the-mill player to a superstar but there was a price to pay. I accept that not every British footballer is given the opportunity to play on the Continent where there is no doubt an edge, at least in technique, but you have to have a certain character and temperament to cope. The nightmare started soon after my plane had touched down. There was a party of officials to welcome me and I felt like a VIP as we zoomed through rush-hour traffic to my hotel. I don't quite know what I had expected, certainly not a palace because, after all, I was a foot-baller coming out to work. But I never expected them to dump me in one of those hotels that gets mentioned in holiday horror stories. The facilities were pathetic.

I might have stayed cheerful if they had made some attempt to provide me with a little company or somebody who spoke the language to help me get around the place for the first few weeks. Jill was back in Wales and I was missing her greatly. I didn't really expect them to have a car for me but it would have been nice if they had helped me get fixed up so that I could get out of what really was a dump. It's strange really: Barcelona were paying me a fortune but were bankrupt in human terms. They used to say in the old days, when there was a maximum wage, that players were bought and sold like cattle and it was at this point that I knew what they had in mind. I felt forgotten and almost banished. I had no friends, I couldn't speak Spanish and it was all a bit disheartening. It was the loneliest period of my life.

I wasn't being singled out for this cold, distant treatment. I've since discovered that it's the usual routine for Spanish clubs who, once they have signed you, feel it is the end of their responsibility. You are treated like property which they own lock, stock and barrel and they make sure you know it. The hotel food was so bad I always ate out. After a few weeks they made a big concession and arranged a sponsored club car for me. Actually, you could have parked it in a dog kennel but at least it had wheels and I could go places.

Perhaps I'm sounding a bit feeble and a stronger charac-ter would have quickly got himself better organised but, as I say, my heart wasn't really in this transfer and I was just out of my depth as a young, mixed-up Welsh boy far from home. Eventually, I realised I had to do something about my life and spend some money to escape my downtown hotel. So I went out house-hunting and fixed myself up with a typical Spanish-looking villa high in the beautiful hills above Barcelona. The view was spectacular and for a time I revelled in my independence and posh surroundings. I figured I had been really smart until it dawned on me that those characteristic wrought-iron bars they have across their windows in that part of the world spelled out that I was in something of a prison. I became progressively more isolated until I lived like a recluse. The other players shot off in different directions after training to do their own thing. Nobody stuck around for a chat or a bite to eat and I had nothing to do but head back home and stare at the four walls of my palace prison. I'm no cook, either, and the most ambitious food I attempted was a variety of toasted sandwiches. It was the only food I had for days on end.

The other occupation to shut out the boredom was sleep. On my days off I could sleep the clock round. To be fair, when Gary Lineker and his wife, Michelle, arrived in Barcelona they tried to help me as much as possible. They invited me out to dinner and round to their house but I felt uncomfortable about going too often because they were a young couple, not long married, and they deserved their own space without me hanging around. I always enjoyed their company but I turned down more invitations than I accepted because I was plain embarrassed.

Things were better on the football side. The training sessions went smoothly and the pre-season matches were a dream. I was knocking in goals at a steady rate and the Spanish fans loved it. They welcomed me very warmly and whenever I became depressed and lonely, I reminded myself that I had the football to relieve the heartache and frustration. Little did I know what was to come. Once the season started in earnest it was a slightly different story. Gary Lineker hit top form and launched Barcelona's season in a spectacular fashion with a string of goals. But as fast as Links scored 'em, I missed 'em

Not a player to be pushed around

Except perhaps by the referee

Hughes, wearing United's green and gold nostalgia strip, confronts Sheffield United's Jamie Hoyland at Bramall Lane

Now it's the man in black blasting at goal

*Back in the more familiar red and certainly in familiar mid-air action as he leaps
for a shot against Wimbledon*

Mark smashes a volley home for United's goal in the 1993 FA Charity Shield against Arsenal

United won the penalty shoot-out after a 1-1 draw with the Gunners. Mark displays the FA Charity Shield with goalkeeper Peter Schmeichel and skipper Steve Bruce

This was the 'miracle' goal by Mark as he held off Craig Fleming to volley a beauty and earn United a last-minute reprieve in the FA Cup semi-final against Oldham on the way to their historic League and Cup double

The United striker scored the last goal of the season to seal a 4-0 FA Cup final win against Chelsea

*A proud and happy moment for Mark with both the Premiership trophy and
Sir Matt Busby, the founding father of the modern-day Manchester United*

Manchester United's first ever League and FA Cup double with the silverware on show at Mark's testimonial match at Old Trafford

Mark and company (Alex aged six and four-year-old Curtis) take a testimonial bow after the match against Glasgow Celtic with a free ride for Xenna

An acrobatic overhead kick from Mark, despite the attentions of Mauro Silva, as Wales sweep to a notable 1-0 win against Brazil at Cardiff Arms Park

and I struggled to match his strike rate. It was a month before I got my first League goal and though the supporters continued to show patience the media started to make invidious comparisons between the two British imports. I know who came off worst. As I explained earlier, I believe there are other things than scoring to be taken into account but the Spanish press didn't see it that way. The storm broke when we played Real Madrid, rivals treated like aliens from another planet, and the critics didn't like my performance. I couldn't believe their vicious reaction.

The season was barely six weeks old and it seemed they wanted a sacrificial lamb at even that early stage. Later I realised that they had turned on me for political reasons. I was a pawn in a battle to discredit the president, who had sanctioned my signing. Terry Venables was too popular to attack and Gary was an obvious success with all his goals, which left me as an easy target and a means of stirring up trouble for the president.

The criticism centred on my lack of goals and my style of play. They began a campaign in which it was claimed that I was too aggressive and more interested in whacking someone than scoring a goal. It was all nonsense but it is possible that my British approach to the game was a little more robust than the Spanish style. It wasn't sly, like that of some of the local hatchet-men, but because it was open it was easy for the media to orchestrate a hate campaign spotlighting the way I played.

I am sure they understood my game but they chose not to, unlike my team-mates, who were always very supportive. They knew that in the game against Real Madrid I had chased all over the park, closing down defenders to deny them space, making tackles all over the field, winning possession and sweating buckets. But the pressmen who were gunning for me ignored that side of my game and just highlighted the fact that I hadn't scored. Gary suited them fine. His game was scoring and, as I explained earlier, he cottoned on quicker than me to what he had to deliver. It was his bag anyway.

The fans were fine and despite the bad press they stuck with me. Whenever I was out and about in the cafés and restaurants in the city they never gave me any hassle, just a pat on the back and a few words of encouragement. The thing about the media criticism which really worried me was that I knew it would all get relayed back home to Britain. I could live with the Spanish papers – after all I couldn't read them – but I was concerned about what was being written back home because it would be read by Jill, my family, friends and, very important this, the English football clubs. I hadn't emigrated for good and one day I had to come back. What worried me was whether anybody would be interested in a foreign flop.

The more I worried, the worse it became. In any sport or responsible job you must have peace of mind to be at your best and I was fast reaching the stage where everything was out of control. It was at this point that I thought of doing a runner, though deep down I knew this would be professional suicide and that I just had to stick it out.

The one big thing I had in my favour was a manager who was a fellow countryman, and Terry Venables was more supportive than I had any right to expect. His head was on the block as well, of course, because he was the man who had bought me and obviously if a manager buys a foreigner in preference to a local player, the player has got to succeed or else the manager is in trouble. I suppose the success of Gary Lineker helped him in that respect but even so he never wavered and stuck with me for as long as he reasonably could. He backed me and always gave me plenty of encouragement. I know a lot of managers who would have cut their losses and kicked me out a lot earlier.

He had me in his office or put an arm round my shoulders at the training ground on countless occasions. He even offered me a break from the pressures so that I could take a trip home to recharge my batteries and take stock of my career. Perhaps I could have helped myself more and taken him up on his advice but I am stubborn as well as awkward when expressing myself and, true to my usual way of doing things, I preferred to suffer in silence.

I made a few trips back home to Wales, of course, and it was on one of those flying visits that I got one of the most significant messages of my life. The information filtered through that Alex Ferguson, who had only recently been appointed manager of United following the sacking of Big Ron, was interested in taking me back to Old Trafford at the first opportunity. It was the best news I had had for ages and I went back to Barcelona feeling a lot happier. In the event, it didn't do me much good as I went into a crisis game for Barcelona against Dundee United in the UEFA Cup.

The feeling locally was that we simply had to win. We weren't really in the Championship race and success in Europe was essential to keep everyone reasonably happy. We had to win in Scotland and we didn't. All hell was let loose in the papers, and then, to make matters worse, in the second leg we lost again, with the decisive goal scored at a corner by the lad I was supposed to be marking. As the critics cast around for reasons they looked no further than me. They had never liked my style and so they hammered me all over again. It seemed as if the Spanish League referees had also been reading the press because it suddenly became fashionable to start clamping down on me. It felt as if I couldn't make a tackle without it being ruled out of order. They had me typecast as a rough player and from where I stood it seemed as if I was their favourite whipping-boy. As you can imagine, it didn't help my overall position.

I was dragging my team down and matters came to a head after the UEFA Cup defeat. It didn't surprise me to receive the summons to the manager's office and this time there was nothing Terry Venables could do to help except suggest I took a breather. This time I thought it would be in the best interests of everyone concerned, including myself, to accept the chop with good grace and bow out for a couple of games. At least I thought it would be a couple of games, but that's not how it worked out. Steve Archibald was on their books and he had been loaned out to play for a smaller club because there is a limit on the number of foreign players Spanish clubs can have in their teams. Anyway, he was summoned back to become Gary Lineker's partner and before I knew where I was Barcelona had cancelled my registration in the Spanish League so the vacancy could be filled by Steve. In effect, I was not only dropped but bombed right out of the picture. I could play for the reserves but no longer in the First Division so I had no chance of getting back into the senior team.

I felt some relief but I was upset, too, and definitely angry. At first I felt Terry Venables had played a dirty trick, but when I recalled how long he had stuck by me and I considered that he also was under pressure to get success from the notoriously fickle Spanish directors, I realised that I couldn't hold him responsible for my plight.

He had never flinched when he thought there was a chance of me making it and he resisted the campaign to get at the president by putting pressure on me. He never stopped helping me and indeed taught me a lot about Continental football. He tried, and succeeded I think, in developing my game and moulding it into a more sophisticated style. He is an excellent coach and I believe England have now got the right man in place to make sure this country is at the next World Cup and also does well in the European Championships in a couple of years' time.

It's a shame that the financial problems he ran into at Tottenham still raise their head every now and again because he is very able and it would be a tragedy for English football if anything should crop up to undermine his position. He took Barcelona in his stride and after playing for England at every international level he has emerged a very experienced and shrewd manager. Tactically, he is good and he is an excellent motivator. Players have the highest respect for him, possibly because he treats them like adults off the park as well as on it.

Even when the screw was being turned on me he wouldn't hesitate to take Gary and me out on the town for a meal in the smartest of restaurants. He is a very worldly man and he expected his players to respond in the right way to a grown-up way of life. But he wasn't a pushover if he felt it necessary to be firm, as he showed with the great German star Berndt Schuster.

You might think Lineker and Hughes are big-name players, but compared with Schuster we were small fry in Barcelona. The German international was almost a megastar but that didn't stop Terry fighting a long and bitter battle with him until it was clear who was the boss. Trouble between the two started when Terry substituted him in the final of the European Cup and Berndt didn't like it one little bit. He stormed out of the ground and from then on he and the boss were on a collision course.

Terry has a strong, some might say mean, streak when roused and he froze Schuster out of the team because in his opinion the player's attitude was all wrong. It was a brave thing to do because the fans loved Schuster and naturally expected to see him play. The fact that I was a replacement didn't ease the pressure on me either.

Schuster was also one from the awkward squad and he refused to lie down. He seemed to settle for the money rather than accept that he would have to move and look for a transfer somewhere else. But then at the end of the season, in one of those typical about-turns which you get in football, Schuster dramatically made his peace with the club to return to the fold and claim one of the foreign places.

This really spelled the end of the road for me. I had played for just one season of an eight-year contract and had ended up with the prospect of going nowhere for perhaps the next seven years. I knew that if they wanted to Barcelona would have been prepared to let me waste away in the reserves. They had shown with Schuster that if necessary they didn't mind banishing a player, however famous, into outer space. I knew I would have to compromise on my contract and be prepared to accept a considerable loss of money because I also knew I couldn't face being out of big-time football.

Naturally, my first thoughts were for home and my agent began to negotiate a sell-off transfer fee with Barcelona. Everton, Spurs and Glasgow Rangers all apparently expressed an interest but, importantly for me, so had Manchester United. A secret meeting was arranged with United chairman Martin Edwards and manager Alex Ferguson but we didn't get very far because it was discovered that if I had come back to Britain at that point I would have had to pay a colossal amount of tax. I hadn't been out of the country long enough to meet the conditions necessary for exemption and I was faced with the possibility of paying both in Spain and England. Financially, it didn't make sense, so my return to Old Trafford was put on ice. I wasn't free but at least there was some light at the end of the tunnel.

A rescue then came from a strange quarter and it changed my whole life.

Bayern Munich came on to the scene to express interest in taking me from Barcelona on loan. I flew home for another meeting with United in an effort to find a loophole which would have allowed me to come to Old Trafford on loan without sacrificing thousands of pounds to the Inland Revenue. I might say United were very persuasive but my advisers concluded that I would be crazy to rejoin United at that point. So back to Barcelona I went to start talks with the German club.

I met their manager, Uli Hoeness, and was impressed by his persuasive efforts to get me into the Bundesliga. At the back of my mind I regarded this latest transfer as treading water until such time as I could return to English football without financial penalty. I only had to last another season to reach the April deadline, which would put me in the clear, so I agreed to sign, prepared to take anything they threw at me in my stride. I knew it couldn't be worse than Barcelona!

Bayern were riding high at the time and playing in the European Cup as the reigning German champions, so I was also boosted by the knowledge that I must still have something going for me to attract such a successful outfit. I prepared for a début against Bayer Urdingen, little knowing that this was a move which was going to put me back on my feet and make me a happy man again. My transfer to Munich succeeded beyond all my expectations. The club were tremendous and right from the word go I just seemed to slot into the scheme of things. Their kind of football suited me and, more importantly, I suited them. My début went like a dream.

I played my usual game, working for the team, trying to pull defenders out of position for the benefit of my fellow forwards and getting stuck in just as I had always done. There was a hard, combative edge to the game which I have always relished but which had proved my undoing in Spain. I could take it and I could give it, which suited me down to the ground.

The fact that I also scored to help win this first game perhaps helped as well, but I had already struck a few chords with the Bayern players. Like footballers back home, they were always ready to take the mickey, especially out of a foreign new boy and I got my share of the leg-pulling. In fact, I hadn't been working with them for very long when they twigged that my skills were not quite as finely honed as their own. One of the training exercises they used to do involved passing the ball to one another without it touching the ground. It's tailor made for cheating because if you want to embarrass someone you give him an awkward ball, or if you want to make some money towards a Christmas party then you introduce penalties for failing to keep the ball in the air. They made me the fall-guy and it cost me plenty of marks, but, strangely, I didn't mind a bit. I was just glad to be involved in the joking and made to feel part of the dressing-room banter. Hoeness, vastly experienced as a German international and World Cup winner, made me feel I was contributing something important to his team. On one occasion my plane for a visit home was held up by fog, but rather than leave me to my own devices he took me home and made me feel very welcome as we got down to some serious football chat. He called my performance world class. I mention it at risk of seeming boastful but it was the significance of being made to feel a key part of his set-up which was the important thing. It was a lot better than the knocking and negative criticism of Spain.

I eventually caught my flight to Manchester where Jill was waiting for me, and we got on with planning our wedding. I was delighted that soon I would have her out with me in Germany and I could live a proper family life. As I said earlier, if I had had that kind of support in Barcelona I might have done a bit better, though I doubt it because, as the German experience confirmed, I wasn't in a football environment which suited me until I had got to Bayern.

Bayern did everything with not just style but a human touch. For instance, within a couple of days of my arrival in Munich there was a brand-new BMW delivered. The hotel was first class and I was made to feel not just important but welcome. When Jill finally flew in to join me the boss was there as well with a bouquet of flowers. It's the little things that count, at least for me!

Uli certainly gave me the five-star treatment for my next game, which was a big Cup tie against Borussia Moenchengladbach. We were both frustrated because it clashed with Wales playing Czechoslovakia in a European Championship qualifier and naturally I had to be released for an important international like that. From Uli's point of view, he was reluctant to release me because he wanted to keep his goal-scoring newcomer in the team, and so he put his mind to work on getting me from Prague, where the game was to kick-off in the afternoon, back for our night game.

He reckoned I had captured the imagination of the Bayern fans and he didn't want their interest to wane. So without telling anyone else he arranged for a car to whisk me to the airport at Prague where a private jet was waiting to fly to Germany. He met me himself at Munich airport and then drove me like mad to the game. Uli hadn't let on what he had arranged to either the players or club officials. He wanted maximum psychological impact, with me appearing as if the old genie had rubbed a magic lamp. It was half-time when we arrived so he kept me out of the way until the teams had gone out again.

Then Borussia scored to go ahead so I was rushed to the touchline to warm up. The crowd didn't twig because I looked very like one of the reserve players and they thought it was him limbering up. There was quite a stir when my name went up on the electronic scoreboard as the substitute coming on and whether it stunned the Borussia players as well I don't know, except to say that within five minutes we had equalised and the game went to extra time. We nicked a winner and everyone at the club was delighted, me especially. I was highly impressed that someone should go to such complicated lengths to have me play in his team. The only disappointment on the day was that we had lost in the afternoon with Wales, but I suppose you cannot have everything.

My loan was until the end of the season. We didn't win any trophies but Bayern felt they had made progress and they wanted to sign me on a permanent transfer, which was very flattering. Clubs back home in Britain were also jumping on to the bandwagon and wondering whether they could nip in ahead of Manchester United. Everton were particularly interested. I think I impressed them with my current form when I played for Bayern at Goodison Park as part of the Football

League centenary celebrations. I scored a goal and had another disallowed. Anyway, the message came down the grapevine from Howard Kendall via Kevin Ratcliffe, the Everton centre-half and a team-mate in the Welsh national side. Rats said Everton wanted to know if I would consider joining them. Rangers and Spurs were also being mentioned as United waited patiently to renew their efforts to bring me home.

United were really the only British club that interested me and, indeed, I had long dreamed of coming back to Old Trafford to spend the rest of my career with the Reds. The only new quantity in the equation was Bayern Munich, who had effectively resurrected my career in my hour of need. I had grown really fond of the place and was enjoying my football again. Jill and our first baby had settled well. We were a family and I seriously wondered about having another couple of years abroad.

I felt a debt to them and Jill had really taken to the life out there. She fancied staying and as she pointed out if we went home then it would be for good. There would probably never be another chance to play abroad and so we both had an inclination to make the most of our lucky break and stick with the club who were so enamoured of me that they were willing to pay Barcelona £1m, a big fee for them.

At the end of the day Manchester United won the tug of war because I also realised that there might never be another opportunity to return to Old Trafford. I had always had this fairy-tale ending written in my mind and this was the factor which tipped the balance . . . that and the persuasive, impressive qualities of Alex Ferguson.

He seemed to me to be the right man for the United job after a succession of managers had come and gone following the great days of Sir Matt Busby. I liked his style from the moment he said that if he had been manager at the time he would never have sold Mark Hughes in the first place and for nearly two years he had made it clear he wanted me back in a red shirt. Even when I was down in the dumps in Barcelona and looking a bad bet to play for anyone, he and Archie Knox had made a point on one of their European trips of calling on me to reassure me that they were waiting for me.

Alex Ferguson really impressed me with his fanaticism for football and in-built desire to win trophies. He seemed well qualified to bring the trophies to Old Trafford. I felt it at the time, and though even the mighty Mac from Scotland had a career crisis four years ago, my judgment has been borne out. The fans craved the Championship in particular and I had noted that when he was appointed to the hot-seat he didn't pursue a safety-first line urging supporters not to expect too much too quickly.

While not sticking his neck out and bragging about what he would do, he adopted a sensible but nevertheless ambitious policy, saying that the League *must* be won for a club of the standing and expectations of Manchester United. It was an irresistible philosophy as far as I was concerned. I had been aware from quite an early stage of my United career that everything about the club is made for greatness and I wanted a slice of it. I certainly didn't want Alex Ferguson looking elsewhere for a partner for Brian McClair while I tried to fix a moment to come home which suited me. Time, tide and Manchester United wait for no man and I sensed that Alex Ferguson was a man in a hurry, patient when he could see a reason for it but not a man who would put off decisions that had to be made, no matter how tough or difficult. He came south as a manager used to success. The relationship between Aberdeen and Glasgow, with its two giants, Celtic and Rangers, is comparable to the relationship between Portsmouth and Manchester: the former is miles away and not everyone is even sure exactly where it is. There is no obvious reason why either place should have a successful football team but the one-time Rangers centre-forward took the Dons to the top. He broke the monopoly of the big two, winning everything, including the European Cup Winners Cup and he also had a spell managing Scotland, a job I believe he could have had for keeps if he had wanted it.

They say that so great was the success of Sir Matt Busby in his 25-year reign that he cast a shadow over all his successors. It wasn't so much that he interfered but that his presence inhibited the men who followed him. I can well understand it in the period immediately after his retirement, when he was still a relatively young man and people like Wilf McGuinness and Frank O'Farrell must have felt he was looking over their shoulder. So it was easier for Ferguson but he also came as a man proud of his own achievements and rather than looking at Sir Matt as a hindrance he pointed him out to us players as a source of inspiration. I know he made Sir Matt feel he was his friend, which must have been nice for the old man after all the gossip in the early years that he had somehow made it more difficult for his successors.

Naturally, Alex Ferguson did not win all his trophies and dominate Scottish football by being a softie. He has a terrific sense of humour and can share the banter with the best of them. He ran a pub in his early days so he knows how the other half live all right and he usually has a smile on his face. As I say, though, there is a hard cutting edge to him and he won't shirk unpleasant decisions if he feels it necessary. I wouldn't call him ruthless but right through his time at Old Trafford he has left a trail of people who might think otherwise.

Soon after his arrival he turned the club's scouting system upside down. It didn't take him long to realise that Manchester City were taking the pick of the local boys and he did not like that one little bit. Heads rolled in the scouting department and it wasn't long before Les Kershaw was brought in to reorganise the whole set-up. Les has a strange background for a football scout in that he was a lecturer in chemistry at the old Manchester Polytechnic before joining United on a full-time basis. You can judge the impact of his work when you note that two years ago United won the FA Youth Cup for the first time in 28 years and that most of the team have been signed as professionals on four-year contracts.

The boss was quite scathing about some of the players he found at Old Trafford on his arrival. He slaughtered Frank Stapleton, my first partner, in his book about his management of United and he had a fair old go at Gordon Strachan over why he sold him to Leeds. He didn't mess about with Norman Whiteside and Paul McGrath either, when he decided he didn't want them around the place. He devastated Jim Leighton by dropping him for an FA Cup final replay. Last season he surprised a lot of United fans by parting company with the popular Nobby Stiles, one of the junior-team coaches and a famous ex-Red, of course. Then only this summer, he shocked our physiotherapist, Jim McGregor, by deciding not to renew his contract after 15 years' service.

He is hardly a soft touch, but then Manchester United matters to him and if anyone falls short of matching that commitment and enthusiasm he quickly runs out of patience. As players, we see his mean streak from time to time and quite often his fiery nature, which can go from sunny to stormy like a bolt of lightning. Everyone talks about him throwing cups and saucers around the dressing-room. Gordon Strachan can vouch for it, but he seems to have dropped that particular party trick from his repertoire these days. That doesn't mean he is any less fearsome when he decides we need a blast. His words and language burn like a blowtorch but I can live with that because I know the man has a burning passion to be a winner. And if you don't have a manager who wants to win things what chance have the rest of us? I knew that if I went back to Manchester United I would be joining a winning team.

So, though we had been very happy in Munich and I was grateful to the Germans for putting my career back on track, we packed our belongings and returned to the club which had launched me.

Chapter Seven

A LIFELINE

I APPRECIATED the lifeline Alex Ferguson had thrown to me in Barcelona but it didn't take me long to realise that life was not going to be a bed of roses. The boss is a demanding taskmaster as he demonstrated in my first season back at Old Trafford in 1988–89 when he put two popular and top-class players on the transfer list. The fall of Paul McGrath and Norman Whiteside sent ripples through the dressing-room as well as surprising many supporters.

I have always rated Paul the best central defender in the country. I remember years ago being asked in one of those typical football-magazine questionnaires to name the most difficult opponent I had faced. I answered Paul McGrath in training, and, though I have played against a few cracking defenders since, I have not changed my mind. So in many ways it was a tragedy for Manchester United that he was forced out and I can tell you there were a few raised eyebrows among the players. Indeed, many fans seriously questioned the manager's judgment and considered that perhaps he should have straightened him out rather than get rid of him. Norman, as a player who had come up through the junior ranks and had this fierce commitment allied to great skill and perception, was also a popular guy with the supporters. His departure was also a shock.

The situation was that things had been a bit lax under Ron Atkinson on the social scene. He took the view that we were all big boys and had to take responsibility for our own lives and that it didn't really matter, within reason, what we did in our own time, provided we delivered on the park. Alex didn't like that kind of relaxed atmosphere. He was the new manager, too, and probably felt he had to impose his own standards as quickly as possible. He didn't like the discipline he found and, characteristically, he did something about it.

Ironically, he is more easy-going these days and maybe more tolerant, though really we probably don't test him. We know what he is like and instinctively you don't push your luck. Everyone was very shocked at the time and we all felt a lot of sympathy for Paul and Norman because they were both well liked and respected as people as well as players. I count them among my friends and can well understand how they started on the slippery slope which led to their downfall as United players.

Their problems started when they both hit serious difficulties with their knees and they were more often than not under treatment. I think Paul only played about 20 games in his last season and Norman a mere half dozen. They had too much time on their hands and they got into the habit of going out for lunch together. One thing would lead to another and I have no doubt that with no match to prepare for there was nothing to tell them when to stop.

It's easy to get into that kind of routine when you are not involved. You feel out of it and neglected. Your team-mates have the buzz of the next game but you have only your injuries to fret about. A few drinks and a lot of chat would dull the pain and I imagine they would feel sorry for themselves and make excuses for each other. It is hard to break a habit that creeps up on you when you are on the outside looking in and eating your heart out. I can well understand how the lads got caught up in a way of life which at the end made a parting of the ways the best result for both manager and players.

I always felt Norman had himself under control and the shock of the transfer saw the Belfast man make a useful contribution at Goodison Park before his knee injuries forced him to an early retirement. The trauma of being kicked out of Old Trafford and the chance of a fresh start also brought Paul to his senses and with perhaps a slightly more benevolent régime under first Graham Taylor and then, ironically, Ron Atkinson he again captured the imagination as the best defender in the game. He always seemed to have an extra gear of speed and he could use it to devastating effect despite his dodgy knees.

He also seems to survive well without much training. I believe he spends his time between matches doing exercise rather than hard stamina work, which would aggravate the state of his legs. From time to time you read about him going missing – indeed, Jack Charlton was tearing what's left of his hair out when his man failed to appear for one of the World Cup warm-up games – but his performances in the States showed that he still has a supreme talent.

Being away from a high-profile club like Manchester United also probably made life easier for him. I think Graham Taylor spirited him away to a health farm to help him put himself back together after his problems in Manchester. You didn't read much about it in the papers, which was good for Paul, but I doubt whether he would have got away with it at Old Trafford. You can't do a thing in Manchester without someone knowing about it and then, bang, it's all over the back pages. I'm not complaining, because if you are with a big club than you have to accept that the media coverage is intensive. You can't have your cake and eat it, as they say!

I just thanked my lucky stars that I had left my own uncertain early days well behind. In fact, when I came back from Spain I had never felt fitter in my life and I have to put that down to the training in Germany. The public conception is that while the Continentals have the edge on British footballers in terms of skill and technique we make up for it with superior fitness and physical strength. My experience playing at home and abroad tells me this is nonsense because the Europeans mostly train harder than we do. I went away as one of those guys who invariably trailed at the back when the squad trained; I returned to find that with no conscious effort I was running along in the leading group. It must have been as big a shock to my team-mates who knew me of old as it was to myself.

I'm not saying that the training on the Continent is harder in itself, it's just that the players there seem to apply themselves better and push themselves harder. Before I went away, if I felt pain I used to think it was time to ease up and I would make excuses to myself, such as running isn't my cup of tea. It's a mental thing really, rather then physical, and I found the European players had an extra degree of commitment which eventually rubbed off on me.

Ever since, I have been a better trainer and, as I say, more often than not helping to set the pace with the front-runners. I feel better for training hard, too. Some players like to hold a bit back in training in case they don't have enough left for the actual match. They consider that the time to really let yourself go is on Saturday afternoon, but nowadays I feel that if I haven't trained well then I cannot perform well. So I came back from Germany a lot fitter and therefore a better player. I had learned a few things, too, though I am not sure whether my technique was any better for the experience of working with and playing alongside Continentals.

The European style can be flattering to individuals because they give you more time. They allow you to receive the ball instead of trying to clatter you as soon as you get it. They are more interested in putting themselves between you and their goal so they invariably let you alone, which means you have the opportunity to be gentle with the ball and stroke it around. Provided you have a reasonable level of skill, it does in fact make you look a better player, hence this idea that the Continental players are more refined. It's just a different way of playing.

For instance, at the World Cup this summer the Irish lads didn't look inferior on the ball to me. They maybe didn't have a Romario, Baggio or Stoichkov but we are talking here about the world's best. I recall thinking when I made my début for Bayern how easy it was. I thought if this is all there is to it then it's going to be a doddle. I hadn't trained for ages either. All that had come to a stop because of the transfer, yet as I told you earlier I scored and got rave reviews.

Mind you, I had a rude awakening in my second game, which was against Stuttgart, when the chunky Guido Buchwald made a point of welcoming me to Germany in a more familiar manner, giving me quite a going over. I watched him with interest when he played for Germany in the States this summer because my last game for Bayern found me facing him once again. I was a new boy the first time, not so ready to take a second helping of punishment. So after he had gone through me three or four times, I just swung round and kicked him. Needless to say, I was sent off having played just 20 minutes of my farewell match. Not a very distinguished swan-song, but happily I brought back an improved Mark Hughes in other areas.

I felt I did quite well in my first season back. I scored 14 League goals and a couple in the FA Cup. The rub was that Brian McClair's scoring had slumped. As I explained earlier, my partnership with Choccy had not clicked, a situation which was picked up by the media, to my disadvantage. I did well for short periods but lacked consistency. Perhaps one of my better spells came just before Christmas when my fellow professionals were voting for their player of the year because I won the PFA Award, which I must say was a big boost and at least bore out that a few other folk considered I had come back a better player.

As I say, the season itself was erratic and we finished 11th in the League, certainly not what the manager, nor indeed the supporters, had in mind when he forked out £1.6m to team me up with Choccy McClair. It was a period of transition, though, and I suspect the boss had had to sell two or three players to get my fee together. It was the season which not only saw the departure of McGrath and Whiteside but also Jesper Olsen, Peter Davenport and Gordon Strachan. Although I had been added to the forward line, the suppliers had gone so that Choccy and I suffered.

It was disappointing to see little Strac go because he was a very creative and entertaining player, just the kind to delight the United following, who like nothing better than a good dribbler. He hadn't lost his skill and technique because that is always the last to go but he was getting short of a bit of pace and he was no longer prepared to go down his wing and get past the full-back on the outside. I think this annoyed the manager, who, of course, had had him at Aberdeen and in the end they both needed a change.

He was given a different role at Leeds, where he became the midfield general. It suited him and he liked the fresh challenge. It was the perfect move for him and he played a key part in not only bringing Leeds into the First Division but inspiring them for the Championship. Don't jump to the conclusion, though, that our manager had sold him on too soon because if he had stayed I doubt whether he would have been half as successful.

Nevertheless, all the departures and the absence of

McGrath and Whiteside had ripped a hole in our squad and when we began to pick up a few injuries the boss had to look to his young reserves. This was the 1988 season of Fergie's Fledglings, as they were christened, and they helped spark a run in the FA Cup which was exciting while it lasted.

The third round brought Queens Park Rangers to Old Trafford for the first of three tremendous tussles. There was no score in the first tie and few gave us much of a chance for the replay at Loftus Road. That was when the kids rose to the occasion in fine style. Tony Gill, who had been in the starting line-up, scored and Deiniol Graham, who came on in extra time, scored for a 2-2 draw and another crack at them in Manchester. This time we had one or two of the injured senior players back, such as Gordon and Robbo, who scored, which with two from Choccy gave us a comfortable 3-0 win.

I began to get my act together and was among the scorers in the next round during an easy 4-0 home win against Oxford. I scored in the fifth round as well, a more important goal this time because it was the only one for us in a draw at Bournemouth. Choccy won the replay for us 1-0 at Old Trafford to give us a reasonable tie at home to Nottingham Forest.

Then our League form overtook us and we suffered a sixth-round knock-out 1-0. We didn't play all that well but we didn't have much luck either. For when Brian McClair forced the ball over the line from Paul McGrath's header, the referee refused to give a goal. That was when our boss took an increasing dislike to Brian Hill, a referee who seemed to haunt us with controversial decisions. We had already gone out of the Littlewoods Cup in dramatic circumstances at Wimbledon, and guess who the referee was? Yes, that's right, our friend Mr Hill was in charge when we came off the field to spark the notorious tunnel incident involving John Fashanu and our Viv Anderson.

I was back in the dressing-room when I heard a lot of shouting and commotion. I went back out and all I could see were players of both teams jammed into a narrow corridor and a lot of talk about how Viv had come to be knocked out cold. He was carried into the dressing-room and slowly it emerged that he had tangled with Fashanu. The curious thing was that Viv had only been on the field for a few minutes as a substitute. It wasn't until the 85th minute that he came on and so it was hardly a case of a long-running feud. Gossip in the dressing-room suggested that the bother between them had involved a girl in the distant past. That turned out to be rubbish. I think it was a case of two people taking an instant dislike to each other and exchanging a few insults on the field which were settled in the tunnel.

Viv was later suspended for one game and fined £750 for directing 'insulting and improper comments' at the Wimbledon player. Fashanu was banned for three matches and fined £2,000 so you can draw your own conclusions as to which of them the FA considered the greater offender. I'll never forget our manager coming back from the FA inquiry to tell us that Fashanu had asked the disciplinary committee: 'Look, would a Dr Barnardo's boy do something like that?' The short answer is, well, yes he might – but it impressed the FA inquiry and didn't improve the relationship between Manchester United and Wimbledon.

The insult to add to the injury was that we were beaten 2-1 at Plough Lane and it was only our second match in the competition. We had lasted a bit longer in the Centenary Cup, which was played very early in the season. We beat Everton and Newcastle before losing to Arsenal 2-1 in the semi-final at Villa Park. Sandwiched between the Cup ties we stuttered along in the League and made a particularly poor finish, losing six of our final eight League games. I was part of the flop finish, scoring only once in that run. In fact, I had scored only three League goals in the second half of the

season. The first half was fine, with the goals coming regularly. I had a spell of five goals in five games and then, after a
blank match, I got seven from nine appearances.

The most memorable part of the season was the little
flurry in the FA Cup featuring the youngsters. I thought at
the time that we might have heard more of them. Tony Gill
had his career ended by injury and none of the others developed as well as hoped, except for Mark Robins who, while
never becoming a first-team regular, certainly made his mark
in some important games before being transferred to
Norwich.

Clearly, at the end of the season we were going nowhere
and the manager decided that he needed to take some drastic
action. He had thinned down the playing staff and during the
summer and the opening month of the following season he
swept through the transfer market like a tornado. He signed
Neil Webb, Paul Ince, Mike Phelan, Gary Pallister and Danny
Wallace for what was then a massive outlay of £7.3m. He had
also tried unsuccessfully for two more, Glen Hysen the
Swedish international, later to play for Liverpool, and winger
Trevor Steven of Everton and Glasgow Rangers fame.

We all gathered for the start of the 1989–90 season feeling
that if cash and activity in the transfer market were anything
to go by then we were in for a great campaign. Naturally, there
were a lot of players looking over their shoulders and wondering if their own particular niche in the team was in jeop-
ardy. The manager hadn't actually bought a striker so my own
position looked reasonably safe. Indeed, I really looked
forward to the season because it was clear from the signings
that, like me, the boss felt we needed to improve the quality
of the service to the front men.

We were excited by the arrival of Neil Webb, one of the
most respected ball-players in the country, who had been
responsible for a lot of the quality in Nottingham Forest's
expressive football. He was always so comfortable on the ball

and I relished the prospect of him dropping his pin-point 35-yard passes into my path. He couldn't have asked for a better start to his United career. He scored a smashing goal as we ran up a 4-1 win against Arsenal at Old Trafford, an exciting start considering the Gunners were the reigning champions. I scored, too, and we were all pretty pleased with the way we had opened the new season with new boys Pallister, Ince and Wallace still to play.

We quickly came down to earth with a bump, for after drawing 1-1 at Crystal Palace we crashed to three successive defeats, against Derby, Norwich and Everton. For poor old Neil Webb it was an even bigger disaster. He had made only four appearances for us when he ruptured his Achilles tendon playing for England, an injury which was to keep him out for most of the season and undermine his career as a United man. For, although he returned towards the end of the season, he was never the same player. I think his confidence was undermined. Deep down I believe he felt he wasn't quite as good as he had been and he got very uptight. He tried to work harder, which was never the strength of his game, and to do that he felt he had to lose weight. He changed his diet and it seemed his mind got clogged up and he became very insecure. Footballers can react in strange ways when their playing careers are threatened, as we saw with Norman Whiteside and Paul McGrath. Neil never had their problem but there was one memorable occasion when he let himself go with a few bottles of wine on a journey south. He wasn't playing but he was in the squad to keep him involved. The manager sent him home but really it was a touch of bravado from Neil, trying to show he could handle everything when, in fact, he couldn't.

Neil had a run-in with the boss later over an England call-up and the upshot of everything was a move back to Nottingham Forest. I look forward to playing Forest again this season following their promotion and I'm glad Neil is back in the swim because he's a good guy who always had a smile on his face.

His injury didn't help our situation, particularly around the turn of the year when Bryan Robson dropped out with a groin strain which wouldn't get better and a hernia was finally diagnosed, which needed an operation, and overall cost him three months of the season. The gaffer had planned his team round a midfield engine of Webby and Robbo, only to find that he had neither for a major chunk of the year.

Neil's accident triggered a final push for Ince and Pallister, who arrived as Webby bowed out. You couldn't imagine two more contrasting characters: Pally so laid back he nearly falls over backwards, while Incey is the non-stop chatterbox I described earlier. It seemed typical of Paul to have his photograph in the paper wearing a Manchester United shirt while he was still a West Ham player. At the time we all blamed the press because we thought they must have conjured up a trick photograph with his head superimposed on to the body of a United man. We were unfair to the paper because it was our cheerful Cockney who had gone along with the idea. No wonder the West Ham fans were upset and gave him such a hard time on his first return to Upton Park last season. Naturally, nothing is ever straightforward with him and his transfer was further complicated by a problem when he had his medical. He had a groin strain which apparently had shown up on his X-rays and he was only signed on a never-never basis with his fee and even his wages paid like hire-purchase instalments.

Still, I wasn't complaining when Paul made his debut at home to Millwall and I scored a hat-trick in a 5-1 win. He is now an integral part of our team and I must repeat that I hope it is another two or three years before he seriously entertains moving to play in Europe – and by that time he might have his little boy in school, so that he will abandon the idea altogether.

Pally had also made a late start to the season but not such a happy one. His opening two games were both defeats and on his début he had given away a penalty. In fact, it looked to me as if his then record fee of £2.3m weighed heavily on him. He felt he had to justify it and the harder he tried the harder it got, because unlike forwards, who can win you games, all a defender can do is stop you losing them. It makes it harder to prove your worth but after a traumatic start there is no doubt that Pally is the best in the business these days. United's tremendous defensive record over the years speaks volumes for the partnership of Pally and Brucey. Steve has unluckily missed the international bus – he should have been capped long ago – but I see Pally as England's resident centre-half for a good few years to come.

The summer signing who came in at the start and who has been a stalwart for Manchester United until his departure this summer was Mike Phelan. Mike reserved the best goal of his career to earn his transfer to Old Trafford. He scored a screamer against us for Norwich the previous season and I'm sure that was when our manager put his name in his book for future reference. Towards the end of his time with us, Mike was not getting regular first-team football, a situation which naturally prompted him to move on, but I have a lot of time for him. When things were going against him, he never let them get him down. He was very upset towards the end of last season when he was made to train with the reserves instead of with the first-team squad and I must confess it was a decision that surprised me. Over the years he more than made his mark with United. He won all the medals that were going, including Championship, FA Cup and European Cup Winners Cup. He was in the team which won the European final against Barcelona and I think there will be a special bond among all the players of that team that will last for the rest of our lives. He was always good for a laugh and I liked him.

Not quite so successful was the final member of that

shopping haul. Danny Wallace made his début at Portsmouth in the Littlewoods Cup and helped us to a good win with a goal. He was injured after four matches and that's how his career seemed to continue – stop-go, forever suffering hamstring strains and the like. He never seemed to me to get to grips with the place. Eventually, it got to him and he became very uptight. You can't play in that state and, with the crowd turning on him, a transfer was really the only solution. On his day, he was a great little winger with a lot of pace and no one could have predicted that he would have such a hard time.

It was a strange season all round. The standard was set on the opening day when Michael Knighton came out in football gear to take part in the warm-up. He had come to the Cliff training ground one day as we prepared for the season to explain his ideas and plans once he had bought the club from Martin Edwards. I've got to be honest and say he was very convincing. I found him a charismatic guy, though I couldn't believe it when he trotted out and proceeded to juggle with the ball in front of the Stretford End. I don't think the Stretford Enders knew what to make of it either. They could easily have given him a hard time but didn't, probably because, like me, they were impressed by his skills. I wouldn't have liked to have gone out in front of 45,000 people to lay on a solo exhibition like that! I often wonder what would have happened if he had pulled off the deal and become the owner of the club. I think we would have had an extra man in our squad, like it or not!

The extraordinary opening set the scene for scoring five against Millwall and then conceding five the following week. Yes, that was the infamous 5–1 defeat against Manchester City at Maine Road. Every time they attacked they scored. Everything they hit went in. Those t-shirts commemorating City's 5–1 victory should all be worn out by now, so often are they worn. The only consolation for me was that I scored our goal, one of my favourites when I jump up and volley the ball while horizontal to the ground. The goal made it 3-1 and I thought we could perhaps fight back but they came straight at us again to make it 4-1 and then it was curtains. It wasn't a very happy day and we certainly didn't enjoy the sight of Andy Hinchcliffe waving to us and our fans wiggling all five fingers. We remembered that for a long time whenever we met up in subsequent matches. The biggest surprise of all was that the manager didn't slaughter us. I think he was in too much of a state of shock and for once lost for words.

We recovered to perform usefully in a few games but we went out of the Littlewoods Cup at home to Spurs and had a black December with a run of four defeats and two draws. Inevitably, the knives were out for our manager and the papers were full of speculation that he would get the sack. Everything seemed to come to a head as we approached the third round of the FA Cup and a testing tie at Nottingham Forest. The papers whipped it up and presented the match as make or break for the boss. Naturally, we took all the gossip on board and realised that it was our biggest game and challenge of the season.

Our fans were fantastic that day. They sang right through the match as if they realised that it needed an extra effort from them as well as us. There was an air of quiet determination in the dressing-room and, despite the fact that Jimmy Hill said we looked like a beaten team in the warm-up, we got stuck in. We had a few players out with injury so a couple of the youngsters, Russell Beardsmore and Mark Robins, were in the side. We won 1-0 thanks to a goal from Mark who stooped to head in a cross from me. You could say we made our Mark that day!

Mark Robins fans probably feel he was never given a real chance at Old Trafford. His problem was that Choccy and myself blocked his way and his opportunities were few and far between. He had a remarkable scoring record, though, hitting goals galore at junior and reserve-team levels. I think the boss was reluctant to drop either Brian or me because he had doubts about Mark's ability to link up with the rest of the team. He was a goal poacher, a very good one, but not every team can carry a player of that kind. Mark finally ran out of patience a couple of seasons ago and it wasn't long before he was banging in goals for Norwich. His goal against Forest was certainly a life-saver as far as our boss was concerned and he became the scoring hero of a Cup run that gave respectability to our season and, possibly, saved the manager's job.

We stumbled along in the League and, at one point in February, we were in danger of dropping into the relegation zone. We were playing fellow strugglers Millwall at the Den and if we had lost we would have dropped into a bottom-three place. I had to go off to have stitches in the back of my head but got on to the score-sheet with Danny Wallace to give us a valuable 2-1 win. We limped along to finish in 13th place but everything seemed to come together for us in the Cup. After knocking out Forest we faced a tricky trip to Hereford, which some saw as a match to produce a shock result, particularly when the day dawned with some of the worst rainfall they had had in the area for a long time. Even the carpark was under water and the pitch made it difficult for our kind of football. We won 1-0 thanks to a goal from my Welsh buddy Clayton Blackmore. I went down the right with Mike Duxbury and crossed for Clayton to drive in a sound shot and get us off the hook.

A lot of people didn't give us much chance when the fifth-round draw took us to Newcastle, a club with great Cup tradition and emerging from the doldrums. It was a real Cup tie and, arguably, the best game Danny ever played for us. He scored along with Choccy and Mark Robins for an exciting 3-2 win. We were made to go the hard way to Wembley, for the sixth round gave us yet another away tie, this time at Sheffield United. Choccy won it for us 1-0 but we were better value than that. Danny was through two or three times without actually scoring and we were definitely the better team on the day, though I say it myself!

Then we had two tremendous matches against Oldham which I have already mentioned, the Latics being our semi-final opponents last season too. Robbo, Neil Webb and Danny were the scorers in a 3-3 draw at Maine Road. Choccy took us to extra time in the replay and then Mark Robins, who had come on in extra time, scored the winner to earn us a trip to Wembley. I failed to score in either game and I put that down to Earl Barrett who was marking me. He's very strong, wiry and quick, and I'm afraid I never really worked him out. Oldham were direct and delivered a lot of good crosses into the penalty area. They were great games and Oldham probably felt they had been unlucky but, as they say, if your name is on the Cup there's not much the opposition can do about it. As our Cup run had gathered momentum, I felt that, subconsciously, we had geared ourselves to it. It was our lifeline to respectability and it just remained to put the icing on the cake by beating Crystal Palace in the final.

We were favourites but, after the up-and-down season we had had, we could take nothing for granted. Palace clearly felt they were in with a chance because, to put it bluntly, they did their best to rough us up and knock us off our stride. We weren't expecting it – who would, from a team managed by Steve Coppell, who is the nicest of guys and, as a player himself, always performed with an exemplary attitude? Ian Wright hadn't let his manager influence him unduly in that respect and he came on as a substitute to shake us up some more and bring them alive.

Robbo and I had scored to put us 2-1 in front when Wright exploded on to the scene as a substitute to score twice. At that point we could see the Cup slipping away. I'm really proud that I was the one to earn us the replay when a centre broke to me and I hit it first time with my left foot across the goalkeeper. We lived to fight another day and this time with a new man in goal. Les Sealey had only made a couple of appearances that season but the boss took the bold decision of dropping Jim Leighton for the replay. It must have caused him a lot of personal agony because we all knew Jim had been his goalie at Aberdeen and together they had shared in a lot of success. The harsh truth was that Jim's form had wavered in the face of our rough passage in the League and in the end teams were playing on his lack of confidence by putting high balls into the goalmouth to intimidate him.

None of us actually thought that the manager would drop him until he pulled him on one side just before the team meeting and then broke the news to us. We all felt for him because he's a lovely bloke. The boss has since said that if he had his time over again he wouldn't make the same decision because it certainly messed up Jim's career. His position at Old Trafford became untenable and in the end he had to go. He's back in business now, even playing for Scotland again, but it's taken him a long time. The manager must have had an idea of what might happen but it didn't stop him doing what he thought was best for the club.

The facts tell you that it was the right decision because thanks to our full-back Lee Martin, who carved his own niche in the club's history by scoring a rare goal, we won the FA Cup and so bought time for Alex Ferguson and gave hope for the future to our supporters as well as ourselves. There had been a lot wrong with the team, especially up front, where our scoring rate was low. I had scored 13 in the League but Choccy was down to a modest five. Perhaps the boss had bought too many players too quickly. It takes time to bed people in at a new club. Some of the signings had come at the last minute and were living in hotels for weeks before they were able to get organised with their own homes. I know from bitter experience how devastating that can be to a player's form.

Nevertheless, we celebrated our Cup victory. After all,

we had done it the hard way, playing away from home in every round – what a fortune it must have cost our fans – and we had shown that we must have hidden depths, albeit well concealed! I think that a lot of the players, like me, must also have pondered on the toughness of our manager. A man who could drop a goalkeeper who was like a son to him clearly had a burning ambition to make a success of Manchester United. He had come through a hard, searching examination of his own character as well and I think we all sensed it was a turning point for the fortunes of the club.

Chapter Eight

REVENGE

THERE is no doubt about the number-one target for Manchester United now. The shame of our poor showing in the European competitions of the past two years has left a burning determination in the dressing-room that we must make an impact on the European Cup this season.

We are proud of what we have achieved on the domestic front with our successive League titles and last season's Double, but we all know that we can't really lay claim to be something special until we have proved ourselves on the Continent. Watching the World Cup on television this summer rubbed salt into a painful mental wound as far as I was concerned. The Irish lads were great but the rest of us were back home, reduced to second-class citizens. There were no Englishmen, Scots or Welsh out there in the States. Have we really sunk so low in the soccer ratings that we can't even qualify for the competitions?

Those who reckon the game in Britain is going backwards need only to point to the ineffectual performances of

Manchester United against foreign opposition for evidence that there is a serious flaw in our game. Of course, we have a ready-made excuse and it is certainly a handicap to have to change your team around to comply with the UEFA rule limiting each squad to five non-English players. The insistence that players from Wales, Scotland and Ireland are foreigners because they have their own national associations is a complication which has given a mixed club team such as ours a tremendous handicap. It has certainly been a major factor in our limited progress of late.

There is, though, the risk of using the problem as an excuse, a ready-made cop-out for our shortcomings, and I believe that the mood in the dressing-room has to change. Management must start thinking ahead and prepare the right personnel, which I know Alex Ferguson is doing, and then those of us at the sharp end must resolve that we are going to do better. I don't think UEFA are going to relax their rules and we have got to concede that as long as England, Scotland, the two Irelands and Wales continue to compete as separate entities we can't expect club teams to have the right to play an unlimited number of 'foreigners' in European competition.

So we might as well get on with it, and I would like to think that Manchester United can show the way. After all, it was Sir Matt Busby who led English football into Europe in the first place, which cannot have been an easy decision to make in the face of opposition from our own Football League. But he defied the authorities to establish a very special tradition at Old Trafford and it soon rubs off on you when you become a United player. We all know about the exploits of the Busby Babes against Real Madrid in the Fifties and then the magnificent European Cup triumph in 1968 by the team which included Bobby Charlton, Denis Law and George Best.

My own generation have contributed too, of course, by

winning the FA Cup against Crystal Palace to qualify for the European Cup Winners Cup in season 1990–91 and win it! Significantly, it was just before the introduction of the five-foreigner rule and so we were able to field our normal League team without being forced to juggle around with other players. It was an unbelievable experience and for me person-ally it gave me a great deal of satisfaction to meet Barcelona, the club who labelled me a flop and where I had spent such an unhappy year, in the final. It was all the more rewarding because the season didn't start on a very good note for me.

Hopes were high in the dressing-room after our victory in the FA Cup and we felt that the new players had now had time to settle into the side and were ready to justify all the money which had been spent. We had proved ourselves in Cup competition, if not in the League where we had finished in 13th place, and a lot of us thought that we could make an important challenge for honours. So it came as a big dis-appointment when I found myself dropped after only three games. I moved on to the bench following a 2-1 defeat at Sunderland and then watched Mark Robins score the goal for a 1-0 win at Luton. After that I couldn't really complain about him keeping his place, and when he scored twice in a win against QPR in the following match I expected to stay on the sidelines.

It seemed, though, as if the boss had me down for the tough away games and Mark perhaps for the not-so-tough matches at Old Trafford. Anyway, I was back for the trip to Anfield, which was unfortunate from my point of view because we got taken apart to the tune of 4-0. This cost me my place in the opening match of the European campaign. United hadn't played in Europe for six years; in fact Robbo, Clayton and I were the only survivors, so I was a bit miffed. I remember feeling that I would have enjoyed being part of the big return against Pecsi Munkas. Balloons were going off and there was a really festive air among the fans. Still, we got a good result, with goals from Neil Webb and Clayton for a 2-0 win.

I got back into the team for the next League game and scored my first goal of the season in a 3-2 win against Southampton. Choccy, Mark Robins and I were all in the team together at this stage. The scoring successes were really Brian McClair and Clayton, who had four under his belt by the end of September. I stayed in the side for the second leg against Pecsi in Hungary. The place is OK but the ground was small and it was very warm. We weren't very adventurous as we were determined to hold on to our two-goal advantage. I was up front on my own, relying on hitting them on the break, which we did quite successfully with a goal from Choccy for a 1-0 win.

The next round brought us the draw of mixed feelings. You don't really want to be playing against your own people in a European competition, and personally the last thing I wanted to do was inflict any damage on my home-town team, though perhaps Wrexham were not complaining too much at the thought of two bumper gates. On the plus side, we felt pretty confident of being able to beat them and make progress. We did, in fact, make it easy for ourselves with a 3-0 win in the first leg at Old Trafford. Choccy and Brucey were on target, and so, too, was Pally with a half-volley from the edge of the box which he is still talking about. He rates it his favourite goal, though, as I keep pointing out to him, he is not exactly spoiled for choice when he runs them all through his mind to select the best!

I twisted and tore fibres at the top of my ankle against Liverpool to miss the return leg. Mark Robins came in and scored in a 2-0 win for a smooth passage through to the quarter-finals. This was a nice feeling because the competition was put on the back-burner for four months, which meant we could concentrate on the other competitions in the knowledge that whatever happened we had Europe to come.

By the time we faced Montpellier in March the FA Cup had been and gone with a fifth-round knock-out at Norwich but we were still going well in the Rumbelows Cup. Our League form was still erratic and we did, in fact, lose two successive League fixtures before welcoming Montpellier to Old Trafford for the first leg.

We gave Archie Knox, our coach, some stick after being held to a 1-1 draw, for he had been out to France and had given us a report that they were not a strong side and that they wouldn't want to compete physically. In fact, they got stuck in like madmen and this was the match which saw the dust-up with my marker, Pascal Baills.

I explained earlier that I was very upset when their players called me a cheat. I accept that I stayed on the ground after I had been knocked down because it seemed to me the best place to be. The danger in that kind of situation is that if you leap up and get involved you can end up being sent off as well. As it was, Baills got his marching orders and they were down to ten men but by that time they had hit back for a 1-1 draw and they defended the position extremely well despite being a man short.

We had made an ideal start after I had got Lee Sharpe away down the left wing. Choccy rifled in his cross to put us ahead after only a minute's play. Unhappily, poor old Lee Martin knocked the ball past Les Sealey as he was trying to control it – which was ironic, because if it hadn't been for Lee's FA Cup winning goal at Wembley the previous May in the Crystal Palace replay we wouldn't have been in Europe. That's the way it goes sometimes and the French were greatly boosted by scoring an away goal which would count double in the event of a draw in the return leg.

Louis Nicollin, the Montpellier president, then made his remark that it would be best if I didn't go to France for the return, and when I saw a huge banner at the airport telling me in no uncertain manner to 'f_ _ _ off' I saw he had a point.

Actually, French television complained and they were made to take it down because it was in the way of their shots of our arrival. Anyway, as I tried to explain earlier, this kind of hostility only serves to rev me up and I looked forward to the match. We all probably play a bit better when we are up against it and we needed to raise our game for this one because the odds were definitely stacked against us.

In fact, we produced arguably our best performance on the way to the final. There was a great atmosphere in their tight little ground but the French fans were a little more subdued when Clayton fired in one of his hammer free-kicks just before half-time. It went through the goalkeeper's legs, which was a bit of a lucky break but it was so well hit that it probably took him by surprise, so all credit to my Welsh pal.

Clayton played a big part in our 2-0 win because he was the player brought down for Brucey to score with a penalty and see us finish the match very comfortably. I felt I had the last say in my running battle with Montpellier because my new marker was sent off! This time it was for spitting at me, not the nicest of habits and thankfully it doesn't happen often. The guy thought the referee wasn't looking but the Austrian official turned round at the vital moment and they again finished with ten men. It served them right as well!

Then we really got a good break as we waited for the semi-final draw, with Barcelona, Juventus and Legia Warsaw in the bag. Well, which one would you rather play? And yes, we got the Poles to leave the two European giants, Barcelona and Juventus, to fight it out. Legia had knocked out Sampdoria, so we knew they were something of a surprise package, but even so it was the draw we wanted and we were all determined to make the most of it when we travelled to Warsaw for the first leg. I think our commitment was obvious because we really pulled out all the stops for a great 3-1 win.

The Poles scored first but Brian McClair equalised straightaway. In the second half I put us ahead and Brucey scored his seventh goal in six games, with only two of them coming from the penalty spot. This was the season which saw him bag a total of 19 goals (11 of them penalties) and had him telling Brian McClair and me that one of us should play in defence and let him have a go up front. It was around this time that Choccy started calling him Empty Head!

Our goals gave us a 3-1 advantage, not bad from the away leg. Yet another opponent was sent off – this time Marek Jozwiak was dismissed for pulling down Lee Sharpe, who was turning in some great performances. As we approached the return leg we realised the tie was as good as won. In addition, we had just lost in the final of the Rumbelows Cup and we were all a bit shaken, so we played it safe and came through with a 1-1 result that put us into United's first European final for 23 years. But what made it particularly special was that this was the first season that English clubs were allowed back into European competition for five years following the ban imposed after the Heysel tragedy and here we were making an impact. Many people felt we would have fallen behind in terms of European football but the results suggested otherwise and we were all proud to be reminding everyone that our clubs had had a good record in Europe before the Liverpool disaster.

For me the wheel had turned full circle with Barcelona, who were to be our opponents in the final to be played at the Feyenoord Stadium in Rotterdam on 15 May, 1991. It was a newspaper dream and I immediately became the centre of stories suggesting that for me it would be all about revenge. At first I tried to play it down because really the past is the past and there had been faults on both sides. Deep down, though, I welcomed this chance to put the record straight and show not especially the Barcelona club, but the Spanish fans and especially the media people who had slaughtered me that in the right team I was a better player than they thought.

I wanted to show the football fans of Barcelona the real

Mark Hughes, not the one booted out of town as a flop. Although I have outlined what I considered a raw deal, I have never blamed Terry Venables or the club because it was out on the pitch where it really went wrong. I wasn't scoring goals so, end of story, I had to go, never mind the reasons. I always knew I was a better player than they had seen. I hadn't done justice to myself and here was a heaven-sent opportunity to balance the books. Without wishing to be big-headed about it, I knew I could do it because by that time I was a better player. The Barcelona experience had, in fact, matured me quite a lot, I was also settled with a loving home life, which a person like me needs, and I had regained my confidence.

All the memories of my Spanish nightmare came flooding back and just made me all the more appreciative of my return to Manchester United and the faith Alex Ferguson had shown in bringing me home. We had struggled for a little while after my return but winning the FA Cup the previous year and reaching the final of the Rumbelows Cup as we progressed through Europe had been solid proof that we were gelling as a team. You always know when you are playing in a good side. There is just a feel about it and the balance is good. You respect the men behind you because you know they won't frustrate you by letting in goals faster than you can score them and when you have good, strong men in the middle of the park you know you are in with a chance up front.

We were developing fast as a team with the big-money signings all starting to deliver and Robbo taking on a new lease of life. England had just dropped him but he seemed to take that as a personal spur to produce more for United. Lee Sharpe had emerged as a really outstanding player and had made my job a lot easier with his direct running and quality crossing. The goals had been flowing again and despite all the grumbling about my partnership with Brian McClair there hadn't been much wrong with it that season. Indeed, in all competitions we reached 40 as a partnership before the season was over so there was a great deal of confidence flowing through the whole team. This was a great year for some of our unsung players, too. Mike Phelan had performed well and I think Clayton Blackmore at left back had probably been our most consistent player of the season. Both left on free transfers this summer but this was their year and as we waited for three weeks for the final we felt we had it in us to win.

A few of the players who had once been my team-mates at the Nou Camp were still around but that didn't help us a great deal because they had a new manager in Johan Cruyff, the former Dutch international. Our manager had one or two tricky selection problems to sort out, mainly to choose between Mike and Webby for the third midfield place. Mike got the job, another bitter blow for Neil, who was starting to have a rough ride. It hit him hard and after that, deep down, I don't think he ever forgave Fergie. Choccy was given a key tactical role to mark Ronald Koeman, the Dutch star who wrecked England's hopes of qualifying for the last World Cup. Choccy did an extremely good job and his man only got into the game very late when he scored a consolation goal from a free kick, which you could hardly hold Brian responsible for.

The team for the final lined up as follows: Sealey, Irwin, Bruce, Pallister, Blackmore, Phelan, Ince, Robson, Sharpe, McClair and Yours Truly! My first impression as we approached the Feyenoord Stadium was that our supporters were there in overwhelming numbers. They started singing well before the game and though the day was rainy they maintained their encouragement right through the match. There were explosions and coloured smoke around the ground as we came out but that was the Barcelona support's only real contribution because they were well beaten on the shouting front. As we warmed up I looked across at the Barcelona players and some of them were shivering. Whether it was the cool rain or nerves I'm not sure, but I began to think perhaps they didn't fancy the match as much as we did.

The early exchanges were fairly even except I thought they kept the ball better than us. Their accuracy of passing was just a shade better. Nevertheless, when Pally put Choccy clear through the middle for him to shoot over the bar, it showed they were not infallible and that there could be opportunities for us. We gradually settled and finished the first half, I reckon, looking the stronger side. The boss didn't say a lot during the break except to urge us to get a goal while we were on top. We made our breakthrough about 20 minutes into the second half. Robbo, who had really got to grips in midfield with a very forceful performance, floated a free kick forward after I had been brought down by Alexanco. Steve Bruce met it well with a header sailing towards goal when I nipped in to give it the finishing touch and UEFA officially credited me with the goal. I almost wish I hadn't touched it because Steve has gone on about it ever since and tells everyone that I pinched the goal off him. He can't really be serious because he knows that you can't leave anything to chance. I wasn't to know whether there was a defender intending to whip the ball away and so I made sure.

He got his share of glory anyway. All the other players ran over to him and not me, which tells you who they thought was the real hero. So I was delighted when I was able to make an undisputed contribution eight minutes later to put us further ahead. Again, it was Robbo who created the opportunity with a nice little ball chipped over the defence. Their goalkeeper came racing out but I was able to get to the ball first. I skipped past him but had knocked it wider than I wanted to leave me with what was admittedly an empty goal but a very narrow angle. No time to think, though, and I hammered the ball into the back of the net. People ask me why I hit it so hard instead of approaching the situation with more care and rolling the ball into goal. The short answer is that I don't know why except to say that, as with Steve's goal,

I always like to make sure. I think, in fact, there were a couple of defenders racing back on this occasion so my instinct was right. When I watched a video of the match later and Brian Moore was describing the goal in his commentary he said as I was taking the ball wide that I had lost my chance to score. It wasn't quite as memorable a quote as the 'they think it's all over – it is now' at the end of England's World Cup victory in 1966, but for me it comes close.

Koeman scored one of his free-kick specials with the help, perhaps, of a rather late move by Les Sealey who, by this time, was feeling the effects of the knee injury he had received in the Rumbelows Cup final. His knee had opened up again after one or two dives and if the game had gone into extra time he would probably have been substituted. Barcelona put him under pressure in the last few minutes and we had some hairy moments, especially when Pally and Les had got dragged out of position for the ball to come across and give Brian Laudrup what seemed to be the chance of an open goal. He sidefooted it only for Clayton to come racing into the picture and clear it off the line. We all owe him a great deal for that little rescue act. The Americans are always giving awards for 'Most Valuable' this or that. Clayton deserved one for the Most Valuable Moment of the Match. Not long afterwards the final whistle went and we were the new holders of the European Cup Winners Cup.

Some might say that Barcelona were below par on the day but I'm having none of that. They won the European Cup the following season so you can't underestimate them. I missed out on a lot of the immediate celebrations. I wanted to stay out on the pitch to soak it all up but Gary Newbon dragged me into the tunnel for a television interview. There is a historic photograph which was taken of all the team and substitutes with the newly presented cup with one player missing. No prizes for guessing who. Then, to add insult to injury, Cruyff came walking up the tunnel and Newbon immediately switched horses and chased after the Barcelona manager to interview him. He left me looking and feeling like a big lemon – not exactly the kind of ending I would have scripted for your scoring hero!

Later, a couple of my pals from my days at the Nou Camp, Urbano and the goalkeeper Zubizaretta, came knocking on the dressing-room door to congratulate me, which I thought was really nice. The man marking me, Alexanco, was there in my time but hadn't played because of a bad knee injury. I was, in fact, surprised to see him back in the side, though he wasn't there at the end, having been substituted soon after the first goal. Barcelona also finished with ten men when six minutes from the end Nando was sent off for a professional foul on me. We had made a habit of finishing our European games against teams a man short, something that people might remember when they are having a go at the discipline of Manchester United.

Back at the hotel we had quite a party, as you would imagine, and then it seemed to be one big welcoming do after another. The fans who had been at the game gave us a great send-off from the airport in Holland and there were more people waiting for us back in Manchester. The motorcade went from Manchester airport into the city centre. I shall never forget that as we reached Deansgate it was getting dark and there were constant flashes from cameras, which made a spectacular backdrop for our ride through town. The parade was expected to last two hours but, in fact, it took us six hours to get through the crowds.

The fans went wild, not just because we had triumphed in Europe, notable though that was, but because they could sense that we were a team gathering momentum and reaching the stage where we could reasonably expect to challenge consistently for honours. Our success in Europe had been backed up by a greater consistency in the League and, indeed, we finished in sixth place – a considerable improvement on the previous year's 13th. It might even have been higher but for our preoccupation with the two finals in the last month of the season. For instance, we lost both League games before Rotterdam with our minds undoubtedly straying to foreign fields.

We had certainly shown good form in the Rumbelows Cup after an easy start against Halifax, beating them 5-2 over two legs. The next round brought Liverpool to Old Trafford but goals from Sharpey, me and Steve Bruce with a penalty saw them off quite comfortably, 3-1. Then we had a real tough one and surprised even ourselves by running up a 6-2 win at Arsenal. Lee Sharpe scored a hat-trick, which, with goals from Danny Wallace, Clayton and me, saw the Gunners shot down in spectacular style. It was the match which saw Sharpey's career come together again after a hard time with injury, even if he would run into more problems the following season. It was also satisfying to hit the Gunners for six after being beaten by them at Old Trafford in the League earlier in the season in a game which featured that infamous 'handbags-at-dawn' row. Denis Irwin, who wouldn't hurt a fly, was kicked by Anders Limpar, who ran off chased by two or three of our players. In my view, it looked worse than it was. There was a lot of pushing and shoving and quite honestly it was all over before I realised what was going on. But then most of the incidents like this go over my head. In fact, I get asked pointedly after a rumble: 'And where were you when we needed you?' Perhaps I'm just slow on the uptake but I find it hard to concern myself with other people's problems.

The boss fined Denis, Choccy and Incey. Arsenal even fined their manager, which was very unusual. Perhaps they were trying to impress the FA but it didn't really work because they had two points deducted while we lost one. I'm glad it didn't stop Arsenal winning the Championship because they were the best team that season and they wouldn't have deserved to have missed out on the title as a result of a skirmish like that.

After knocking out Arsenal I scored in a 1-1 draw at Southampton and then hit a rare hat-trick in the replay for a 3-2 win and a semi-final place against the old enemy from Leeds. As you might expect, we had two terrific tussles. Lee scored and I got one to take a 2-1 lead to Elland Road where Sharpey again terrorised Mel Sterland to score the goal in a 1-0 victory. We had to wait a couple of months for the final and when we found it was against Sheffield Wednesday we thought we were home and dry. They were in the Second Division and after knocking out Liverpool, Arsenal and Leeds we assumed we had done the difficult bit.

It just goes to show how dangerous it is to make assumptions. We failed to perform. I think we all had a poor game in a match which saw us beaten 1-0. The most exciting piece of drama came when Les Sealey went down with a badly gashed knee and ended up on the brink of thumping Jim McGregor. As soon as our physio saw the injury he wanted him to come off. It was a bad one. I went to have a look but didn't stay for long because you could actually see the bone. Les wasn't going to miss a moment of Wembley, though, and got quite angry, refusing to leave the field. There was a bit of a scene and in the end Jim just let him get on with it. He bandaged him up and then he had stitches after the match. An hour later he was in a heck of a state, shaking and in a wheelchair. The doctor said later that, if he hadn't gone to hospital at that stage, he could have died, so rapidly was the infection taking him into shock. Les, perhaps because he had had to wait a long time for his run in the first team, never likes to give up the ghost. I remember one match against Sunderland when he collided with a goalpost. He was lying there, moaning and groaning and he looked ready for the stretcher. Brian McClair picked up his gloves only for Les to snarl at him: 'Don't touch my gloves.' He should have gone off, as we realised a few minutes later when he should have come for a cross and didn't. There's no arguing with him at times. He will admit that in his younger days he was not the most dedicated of players. There are some madcap stories about him, but no one could complain about his application when he came to Old Trafford. He simply felt honoured to be there. He lapped everything up and loved it. He was a great character in the dressing-room and used to describe himself as our lucky black cat. He didn't do much for us in the Rumbelows Cup final but he did his stuff all right to help us win the FA Cup the previous season and, of course, he saw us through against Barcelona despite his Wembley injury. Some might say that he wasn't really fit enough for a European final but I don't think the boss fancied telling him!

Beating Barcelona more than made up for the disappointment against Sheffield Wednesday. Since then we have had a thin time in Europe. The following season saw a poor defence of our crown. We disposed of Athinaikos in the opening round but lost 3-0 against Atletico Madrid in Spain with a sloppy performance. We drew 1-1 at Old Trafford when I managed to score but we were never really in with a chance of rescuing the tie. The only consolation in Europe that season was winning the Super Cup by beating Red Star Belgrade 1-0, thanks to Choccy. Two seasons ago we didn't get any further than the opening round of the UEFA Cup. We had a goalless first leg against Torpedo Moscow and, after another goalless match in the return, went out on penalties. Last season was little better . We started convincingly enough with a 3-2 win against Honved in Budapest and beat the Hungarians in the second leg at home.

But then came the disaster against Galatasaray when we made a great start in the first leg at Old Trafford to go two goals up in the first quarter of an hour, only to find ourselves falling behind and fortunate to see Eric grabbing a late equaliser for a 3-3 draw. We just seemed to panic. We lost our shape and discipline. We very nearly lost the match and we could hardly expect to make progress after getting into such a terrible mess against an ordinary side. Naturally, the Turks shut up shop in Istanbul and held us to a goalless game which let them knock us out on the away-goals rule. I was dropped for the second leg and it's difficult for me to say that we would have won if the gaffer had kept me in the side. He had a tricky problem because he was not very happy with the performance of the defence in the first game and he brought Denis Irwin back. That meant another 'foreigner' had to drop out. It could have been Roy Keane but Robbo was struggling with an ear problem and needed cover in midfield so I became the odd man out. At the same time, I had scored in each of the two preceding games and we only needed one goal to win. I didn't throw a wobbler, though, because I'd worked the situation out for myself.

The atmosphere was incredibly intimidating for the fans as well as the players and although we were disappointed to fail again in Europe, I couldn't help feeling a certain sense of relief simply to get back home still in one piece. We had our two other trophies as compensation but there is no doubt that Europe is now our number-one ambition. As my partner, Eric, says: 'I believe that Manchester United can now go on to become the Kings of Europe. Why not? If you don't have the ambition, you might as well stop your career.'

Chapter 9

Nearly There

ALEX FERGUSON stuck his neck out after our triumph in Europe . . . and nearly got it chopped off!

The boss suddenly decided to lay it on the line and committed us to winning the Championship. At first we wondered if it was the lemonade talking from the celebration party the night before in Rotterdam. I know that what he had to say sobered the rest of us because here he was, the Gaffer, saying in no uncertain terms that United fans had waited long enough for the Championship and that the time had come for us to deliver.

There was an unspoken message for us players, too. It went along the lines that if we weren't good enough then it was time for us to go and make way for people capable of bringing the League title to Old Trafford. We all knew that followers of the club had been waiting for 25 years and that some even thought there was a curse on us winning it. So it seemed in the dressing-room, when we first heard the manager's commitment to winning the title, that he was putting unnecessary pressure on us. Managers are usually wary of outlining their ambitions because words come cheap and you can easily end up looking a right charlie with egg spread all over your face.

Indeed, rivals could say that Alex Ferguson went on to finish season 1991–92 looking something of a boastful big-head, for of course this was the year we faltered on the last lap to finish in second place behind Leeds. There was a lot of talk about us throwing the title away because at one point we were way out in front. Some said we had lost our bottle and that Leeds hadn't won it so much as we had handed it to them on a plate. Certainly, the manager's bold declaration had come unstuck, and in the fever of disappointment at the time there were a lot of folk gunning not just for the manager but for the players as well.

It was a bitter experience and for a little while we were in despair. The feeling was that we would never have a better chance and we had blown it, and I think we all regretted that we had allowed ourselves to be so optimistic at the start of the season. So why did the boss suddenly come out so strongly about what we intended to do that season?

My own view is that he felt deep down that we all needed shaking up, that we had become complacent about the failure to achieve the consistency that wins a League. I think he felt we had enough players of quality to go all the way and he wanted us to know what was expected of us. He had seen us win the FA Cup and follow it up by winning the European Cup Winners Cup, so clearly he had every right to talk about us winning the Championship. He told us that the time had come for a big effort, no messing about. He said the time was ripe for a serious assault on the League and that we had to stand up and be counted. It was what the supporters expected and he explained that he was no longer prepared to shelter us from their demands and expectations. He pointed out that if you play for Manchester United you have to deliver and that there was no reason for us to be afraid. We had proved ourselves in Cup competition at home and proved ourselves the best in Europe in the Cup Winners Cup. The mood as we prepared for the new season was that we should go for it.

And I think we did. We'll go into what went wrong, but overall I don't think we had cause to feel any shame. After all, finishing runners-up isn't exactly a disgrace and and we did win the consolation prize of the Rumbelows Cup with victory in the Super Cup thrown in as well. So it was hardly a flop season, and as we know now it was the stepping-stone to ultimate success and our haul of trophies of the last two seasons.

Going back to the start of the season in 1991, though, we still had it all to do as the manager spelled out the targets. There were to be no excuses this time, and he even brought in three new players to strengthen our challenge. He had picked up Andrei Kanchelskis in the closing weeks of the previous season but a delay with his work permit had limited him to just one appearance. He was raring to go in the new season, though, and with Lee Sharpe missing with the first of his hernia problems there was a golden opportunity for him. Indeed, Sharpey managed only eight League appearances that season and even then his troubles weren't over because the following summer he went down with meningitis. So it was just as well the boss had picked up Andrei.

He also did well when he followed up other reports from abroad to make another bargain-buy at around £500,000 for Peter Schmeichel. Jim Leighton was right out of the picture by this time, and though our lucky black cat, Les Sealey, had been brilliant for us I don't think the manager saw the at times erratic Les as the goalkeeper of the future for United. I have already written about Peter, and, as I say, we were all very impressed when this man-mountain walked into our dressing-room. Not only could he speak better English than Incey, he quickly demonstrated that he could play a bit as well. He was always built to be a goalkeeper.

The third signing came as a bit of a surprise because there hadn't been much discussion in the press about United entering the market for a full-back and it seemed to me that Denis Irwin and Clayton Blackmore had done OK for us. I was pleased for Clayton because sometimes when you are known as a versatile, utility player you get moved around and there is never a regular position for you since you are not regarded as a specialist in a particular position. Clayton had had a good run at left-back, though, and fresh from his match-winning interception against Barcelona I thought he had played himself into the side on a permanent basis. He kicked off in the team, but the arrival of Paul Parker was really the beginning of the end for him at Old Trafford, even though it was another couple of seasons before he actually left the club.

One cannot quibble about the value of the small but pacey full-back the chief picked up from Queens Park Rangers, though, and despite hitting a few early injury problems he quickly made the right-back position his own with Denis Irwin switching to the left. It's been that way ever since and a settled defence has been the backbone of our recent success.

I knew right from the start that Paul would do well at Old Trafford. I knew all about him from bitter experience after coming up against him in my first game for United following my transfer back home from Barcelona. I'll never forget it because it was an emotional return for me and I had a stinker! We were playing QPR and in those days Paul played as a central defender. He likes man-marking opponents and he did a great job on me in that match. We were playing at home but it didn't make any difference to Paul. He is small with a low centre of gravity which makes it very difficult to knock him off the ball. For a little man he has a great leap and his timing in the tackle is immaculate. We call him Buzby after the bird in the telephone advert because he is a real yuppie. He owns a mobile phone which is never out of his ear. I wouldn't be surprised one week if he didn't bring it out with him for a match and leave it behind his goal. I can just imagine Schmeichel shouting in a quiet moment: 'Call for you, Buzby.' Goodness knows who he is talking to but he is the original telephone man who would be lost without his link to the outside world and the real reason behind the privatisation profits of British Telecom.

All three of the new players were in the opening match against Notts County at Old Trafford. I was pleased to get off the mark with a goal and with one from Robbo we won 2-0. Andrei was making his home début and looked to be giving defenders ten yards' start and then still flying past them. We were all taken aback by his pace and though perhaps he had yet to learn the finer points of the English game he was obviously an exciting player destined to become popular at Old Trafford.

But additions to the playing staff were not the only changes for the start of the season. We also had a new coach, Brian Kidd, taking over from Archie Knox. The boss had brought Archie with him as his successful partner from Aberdeen and I should have known what to expect when I read the gaffer had said that Archie worked 'like a beast'. What he really meant was that he worked *us* like a beast!

Archie was a fitness fanatic and after a training session at Littleton Road, our secondary training ground, he would often run the couple of miles back to the Cliff to maintain his own fitness level, and woe betide anyone who tried to ease his way through a session without putting 100 per cent effort into it. In fact, if he thought we weren't training properly he was quite likely to stop everything and say we would all have to come back in the afternoon with a better attitude. He could be quite temperamental about it at times, and on some occasions I used to feel it was him who had got out of bed on the wrong side rather than us. Still, he kept us at it and no team ever won anything without being properly prepared. I always felt he was good for Alex Ferguson, too, because he was quite capable of imposing his own character on events and he was never afraid to disagree if he felt strongly about something. In the long run, a yes-man is no good to a manager because no one can be right all the time and to my mind the best kind of right-hand man is one prepared to tell the boss that he feels he is wrong if that is how he feels.

Their partnership brought success at Pittodrie and we all felt that around this time we were beginning to get our act together as a team under the Ferguson-Knox partnership. It had most definitely come as a huge surprise when Archie had suddenly announced just before the end of the previous season that he was leaving to become assistant to Walter Smith at Glasgow Rangers. This was a real stunner, especially the timing of it because we had just qualified for the final of the European Cup Winners Cup, and, as I say, things were beginning to turn our way. We had just played in the final of the Rumbelows Cup and though we had lost to Sheffield Wednesday it was nevertheless an indication that the Red machine was slipping into gear.

The boss is on record as saying that Archie was very quiet in the dressing-room at Wembley and that he felt it could have been one of the factors behind our defeat. I'm not so sure about that myself, though it's kind of him to find an excuse for us! I know the manager was at a loss to understand how Archie could turn his back on something he had helped build when he was on the brink of reaping the reward for a lot of hard work. I suppose at the end of the day it was a matter of Archie being offered the chance to secure his future in a big way because our understanding was that Rangers had made him a very handsome offer to go to Ibrox. Anyway, he didn't dilly-dally and he was away almost with the announcement of his departure. The timing of it from our point of view could have been better because it was a vital stage of the season with the European showdown in Rotterdam coming up. The boss's first reaction was to let Brian Whitehouse, the reserve-team coach, take over the training and he took the warm-up sessions, with the manager getting more involved in the preparation as well.

Our other coaches were given more responsibilities, such as Brian Kidd, who had been working with the juniors, Eric Harrison the youth-team coach, Bryan 'Pop' Robson, who had come down from the North-east after setting up a school of excellence in the Durham area, and Jimmy Ryan, who played for United in the Sixties before a career with Luton and in America and a spell back at Kennilworth Road as manager.

By the time the season had kicked off the boss had made up his mind about a successor for Archie. He turned away from bringing anyone in from outside and instead handed the job to Brian Kidd. Kiddo will be forever remembered for the goal he scored in the European Cup final of 1968 on his 19th birthday. Could there ever be a better way of celebrating a teenage birthday? Better than blowing out candles, that's for sure!

After playing for United Brian had successful stints with Arsenal, Everton and Manchester City before returning to Old Trafford to work at the grass roots with the club. He started working with the newly introduced scheme for football in the community and graduated to working with the schoolboys who came to the Cliff in the evenings for coaching at the club's centre of excellence. From that he became increasingly involved in the recruitment of youngsters and he played an important role when Alex Ferguson decided soon after his appointment as manager that he wanted to reorganise the scouting set-up. I think he felt all the best youngsters from the Manchester area were going to Manchester City and Brian was one of the people who stopped the drift. I don't think it is any coincidence that this was the season which saw Manchester United win the FA Youth Cup with an outstanding crop of youngsters who had been brought to the club by the new régime.

I know the boss was so impressed with them that he gave most of the team four-year professional contracts, which I think is probably unprecedented. I am sure you will hear more from them. Indeed, they are starting to knock on the door now and it was significant that five of them figured in pre-season games this summer. Keith Gillespie, a Northern Ireland winger played in place of the injured Andrei Kanchelskis. Chris Casper, son of Frank Casper the former Burnley player, also played regularly, with other appearances from David Beckham, Nicky Butt and Simon Davies. But for a bad knee injury, I am sure Ben Thornley would have been in the squad and there are other names to make a note of, such as Paul Scholes, an exciting midfield dynamo.

These lads represent some of Kiddo's early work for United so no one begrudged him his promotion to take charge of our pre-season training. Brian Whitehouse had gone back to work for Ron Atkinson in the Midlands and, while there were other slightly more experienced coaches on the staff, Kiddo was a popular choice. I would describe him as a players' man and he got to grips with the job very quickly. It must have been difficult for him in the early days but he soon impressed us with the organisation of his training routines and the planning behind them. He revealed a deep insight into coaching and also introduced some of the latest thinking on fitness techniques involving diet and liquid intake. There have been big changes in football in the area of fitness preparation and Brian has shown himself right on the ball. We are all much more aware of the need to eat and live healthily, away from the game. Kiddo has really got himself involved in the latest developments and I know that during the close seasons he has spent time studying the methods used at places like AC Milan, Bayern Munich and Ajax.

As we set sail to try to live up to our manager's high hopes for us we listened carefully to our new coach and we couldn't have asked for a smoother start. Indeed it was October before we lost our first game! After beating Notts County with Andrei the star supplying the crosses for both goals, we impressed with a 1-0 win at Aston Villa thanks to a penalty from Brucey. I always like playing at Villa Park. It's a good ground and under floodlights it is particularly handsome with a great atmosphere. They hit us hard and tested us physically, but it was around this time that we started to play with a little more steel in our game. As I explained earlier, you have to stand up and be counted in certain games and this was one which saw us give as good as we got. We drew goalless at Everton, but no one was too worried about that as we quietly established ourselves as front-runners. We didn't play very well but Big Peter in goal was showing that he looked like settling quickly into the English game.

A one-goal win at home to Oldham with a late goal from Choccy was our fourth successive clean sheet, surprisingly enough the best run for ten years! Peter wasn't too pleased with his performance, though, in the next game when he let a cross from Gary Speed sail over his head for Lee Chapman to give Leeds an early lead at Old Trafford. Robbo got a late equaliser for us and impressed the boss so much that he pleaded with Graham Taylor not to give him any more England caps. He reckoned Bryan had been coming back from international duty with so many injuries that he wanted him spared to concentrate on our Championship challenge. I'm not sure what Robbo thought about that one, except to say that our captain was playing as if time was no longer on his side for the League title – which, of course, it wasn't – and he was playing out of his skin.

Later, we would come to regret not taking full points off Leeds, but it didn't seem so important at the time, especially when we went to Wimbledon a few days later and came back home with a satisfying 2-1 win. Clayton and Pally got the goals but it was the way that the boss juggled the team which attracted most attention. I played on my own up front with Paul Parker used as a sweeper, and it worked well. Perhaps encouraged by results after making a few changes, it was a policy we would hear more about later in the season, though in slightly more critical tone. Neil Webb had played well at Selhurst Park and was also prominent when we trounced Norwich 3-0 with the help of a three-goal blast in eight minutes from Denis Irwin, Choccy and Giggsy.

I got a new partner for the trip to Southampton with Ryan playing through the middle alongside me. He was still only 17 but the Saints found him difficult to contain and he was involved in the move which saw me get a welcome goal in a 1-0 win. We were fairly quiet in Greece against Athinaikos for a goalless first leg as we began our defence of the European Cup Winners Cup but we exploded into scoring action for a 5-0 win at home to Luton. I got the final goal to make it the biggest victory in Alex Ferguson's reign as manager and the bookmakers responded by shortening the odds to make us 13-8 favourites for the Championship. Choccy had been left out for this match in another of the manager's tactical switches but came on for the last half-hour to score twice in three minutes.

We then had our first glimpse of Dion Dublin as he led Cambridge into action in our opening round of the Rumbelows Cup. He did OK and alerted our people for a subsequent transfer, though he was on the receiving end of a 3-0 defeat in a game dominated by Giggsy with his runs down the wing. We were going well on all fronts and the next match saw Ryan and me team up together as strikers again. Giggsy was becoming something of a good-luck charm for me because I scored again, along with Robbo, for a 2-1 win at Spurs. This meant we had reached the first quarter of the season with a six-point lead in the Championship race. We had improved our scoring rate to grab 18 goals from ten League fixtures with only three scored against us. No wonder people were starting to talk about this being the year for Manchester United to come good!

We polished off the Greeks at Old Trafford before a disaster at home to Liverpool. Not only did we let our old rivals off the hook by drawing 0-0 after outplaying them, but I got myself sent off, no thanks to David Burrows either! I was supposed to have head-butted him after we had become entangled as we chased a ball out of play. I felt he had held me down and we got up for one of those eyeball-to-eyeball confrontations. I put my face forward as you do in that kind of situation. I didn't make any contact but he went down holding his face, and I was not very happy with him at all.

We picked up a draw at Cambridge. Dion scored for them, which no doubt helped put his name in Alex Ferguson's book for future reference, and it saw us progress into the next round of the Rumbelows Cup. A similar 1-1 draw at home to Arsenal wasn't exactly ideal, but it was nothing like the black week to follow. First we cut our own throats with a first-leg 3-0 defeat in Spain against Atletico Madrid and then we went across the Pennines to Sheffield Wednesday for our first League defeat of the season. We came from a goal down for Choccy to score twice and give us a 2-1 lead. We fell away in the last 20 minutes for Nigel Jemson to score twice and leave us with a 3-2 beating. I felt bad about it because I was serving the first part of my two-match suspension.

I missed the next League game as well, though at least we got back on the winning track by beating Sheffield United 2-0 at Old Trafford. We also knocked Portsmouth out of the Rumbelows Cup, though we didn't fare so well in Europe. I got the goal in a 1-1 draw against Atletico but it wasn't good enough to make up for the away leg and it had been a short-lived European campaign. Incidentally, the scorer for Madrid was Berndt Schuster, my old buddy from Barcelona. Still, we managed to beat Red Star for the Super Cup, though whether the Belgrade team were in the right mood in view of the troubles in Yugoslavia I'm not sure.

Our scoring ability came under fire following a goalless derby at Maine Road but, perhaps with alarm bells ringing, then launched into a run of six wins and knocked in a few goals in the process. We dug in at the top of the League by beating Crystal Palace, Coventry, Chelsea and Oldham. We scored four against Coventry and six against Oldham as well as knocking the Latics out of the Rumbelows Cup. The stage was set for a mighty clash with Leeds at Elland Road just after Christmas. We seemed to be heading for full points with a goal from Neil Webb, but ten minutes from the end Pally brought Gary McAllister down to concede a penalty, which was converted by Mel Sterland. I enjoyed the game because it was a do-or-die bid by Leeds who knew they had to get something out of it to stay in the race. Leeds were emerging as the main challengers to our hopes. We still had two games in hand but the draw pegged us back and it seemed we were still reeling when we crashed to our most embarrassing defeat of the season. We came up against a vibrant Queens Park Rangers on New Year's Day and were well and truly hammered 4-1. The fact that I got our goal, my eighth in a run of nine games, was little consolation and all hell was let loose, with people suggesting we had been on a New Year's Eve binge and were suffering from hangovers. It was all nonsense. The manager isn't daft. He took us away to an hotel, despite it being a home game, and after a meal we were all in our rooms by 8.30.

I can't give you any explanation, except to say that QPR played particularly well and it was just one of those days when absolutely nothing went right for us. It was our heaviest defeat for a long time and the first time the London club had ever won at Old Trafford. We were totally outplayed. The hero for Rangers was Dennis Bailey who scored a hat-trick. No disrespect, but I haven't heard much about him since!

A week later we probably made an even bigger mistake. We knocked Leeds United out of the Rumbelows Cup with a 3-1 win at Elland Road. It was lovely to see my pal Clayton scoring along with our wingers but it was a result which was to have significant repercussions as the season progressed. And, as if we hadn't hurt ourselves enough, we went to Leeds again a week later and aggravated the situation by knocking them out of the FA Cup as well. I scored the goal which did the damage but looking back I think it probably damaged our own Championship chances more. The trouble was that, while landing ourselves with extra games, we had freed our main title rivals to concentrate on the League without any Cup distractions. Later in the season we ran into a real fixture jam while Leeds were able to pace themselves with a relatively easy finish. They took full advantage and timed their finishing sprint beautifully.

We were not to realise all this at the time, of course, and we certainly enjoyed our run to Wembley in the Rumbelows Cup. We soon came to grief in the FA competition. We brought Southampton back to Old Trafford only to lose the penalty shoot-out after a 2-2 draw. It was a happier story in the Rumbelows, as I've said. We had a tough, goalless draw at Middlesbrough in the first leg of the semi-final but came through 2-1 after extra time at Old Trafford with goals from Ryan and Sharpey. This took us through to our fourth Cup final in three years and we made amends for our previous season's Wembley defeat in the competition by beating Nottingham Forest 1-0. It was a classy game. Forest always play sound football and give you a chance to play as well. Choccy got the goal and was the sponsors' man of the match.

It's always a thrill to win at Wembley, especially so in this season as the League title slowly slipped away. The slide started with a run of draws as our scoring rate slumped. Relentlessly, Leeds drew level and we were reduced to banking on our games in hand. We lost ground when we went down 1-0 at

Nottingham Forest in the League. It was only our third League defeat of the season but it saw Leeds take a two-point lead at the top of the table. Goalless draws followed at home to Wimbledon and at QPR before we came to scoring life again with a 3-1 win at Norwich. We had lost our consistency, though, and we could only draw 1-1 with Manchester City in the home derby. We managed to win our home match against Southampton but then the roof fell in and we lost our way. We should have done much better than a 1-1 draw at Luton, a team struggling to stay in the division. Forest came to avenge their Wembley defeat by winning 2-1 and raise the issue of whether there was a curse on the Championship coming to Old Trafford. Our goal-scoring had gone to pot and the defeat meant we had only one game in hand on Leeds with our rivals one point ahead. The chips were down and they were going cold! We crashed at West Ham against a team who were already doomed to relegation. The boss described the Hammers' performance as obscene and posed the question of why they hadn't played in their other games as they did against us to avoid the big drop. I think Billy Bonds, their manager, was embarrassed.

We were losing ground rapidly now. We had played our game in hand and Leeds were still a point in front. It was all over a few days later when Leeds won at Sheffield to leave us playing at Liverpool, of all places, later in the day, knowing that we had to win to give ourselves even the slimmest of chances. It was not to be and a 2-0 defeat meant Leeds were the victors. I scored twice in our last match to help beat Spurs 3-1. How I wish I had been able to get those goals during our run of draws - they could have made all the difference.

It was the signal for the inquests to open. The finger was certainly pointed at me as a striker whose goals had dried up somewhat in the second half of the season. Choccy had done well with his goals but without wishing to deflect the blame I think we were also relatively short on scoring support from

157

the rest of the team. Choccy and I were the only players in double figures. The next best scorers were Andrei and Brucey with five apiece in the League. The manager also came under fire. Some critics felt that he had tinkered with team selection too much and that he had changed the team around too often, especially as we drew near to the finishing line. I hadn't been best pleased myself when he left me out of the League game at Forest in March. He felt my scoring had dried up, which was true enough, but I thought it was the wrong game for me to miss. Forest had been playing Nigel Clough with Des Walker in central defence. I would have expected Walker to take Giggsy, which would have left me up against Nigel, and I reckon I could have done well against him. He's not the biggest of fellows and it was no consolation to find the team losing the match.

I think we were all on a learning curve, though, manager and players alike, and I put our failure down to a combination of circumstances. The biggest single factor was the situation which saw Leeds with their fixtures spaced out while we had to tackle three games in six days at a vital stage of the season. I had thought that the main reason for the introduction of the Premier League was to avoid this kind of pile-up but they still haven't slimmed down the division. We all got tense over those last few weeks. It wouldn't be fair to say we bottled it but we did sense the title was slipping away from us and we probably did get a little nervous. At the end of the day, we had too many big games with not enough rest in between. The pitch at Old Trafford didn't help us either. Our game is to pass the ball about quickly and accurately. We like to probe and pick holes in the opposition defence but our ground cut up so badly that our passing went to pot – as in potholes! Teams came to stop us playing on the last lap and we lost the quality on our bumpy pitch to get the better of them.

This isn't a moan, just an attempt to supply a few answers to the questions flung at us by fans who had seen their dream turn into a nightmare. All credit to Leeds, who had kept their nerve. They had been happy watching us play twice a week in the closing stages and they made the most of their opportunity. At the end of the season we all felt sad and drained but consoled ourselves with the thought that overall, to finish League runners-up and win a Cup hadn't been too bad an effort. It didn't seem good enough at the time but, as events have since proved, I think we all learned a lot from a very bitter experience and the lessons provided a foundation for our success of the last two seasons. As the manager is fond of telling us: sometimes you have to suffer pain and agony to earn the rewards.

Chapter 10

At Last

GIGGSMANIA seems almost to have taken Manchester United over. I have already paid tribute to Ryan Giggs the footballer but we are dealing now with a phenomenon, a player who has become not just a sporting hero but a pin-up teen idol. Older fans tell me they haven't seen anything like it since the days of George Best, who was probably soccer's first cult figure to transcend normal sporting boundaries.

There were some amazing scenes on our pre-season trips to Ireland and Scotland as we prepared for this season. I am fairly used to fans being around to collect autographs, because, let's face it, Manchester United are a pretty famous club and recently we have been collecting a few pots, but this was something different. The girls besieged our hotels and went potty trying to get close to Ryan, screaming whenever he appeared and mobbing him as he came out of the lift or whenever he got on or off the team bus. He is young, of course, and so the fans are mostly young girls, who naturally shriek a lot and tend to become a bit hysterical, though I have noticed that there are a few slightly more mature ladies who perhaps want to mother him. Lee Sharpe is another target for the girls, but it's really Ryan who is top of the pops.

When we played at Shelbourne in Dublin one lass jumped over the fence and planted a kiss on Ryan's cheek as he prepared to take a corner kick. It just seemed to sum up how popular he has become. There is no getting away from it for Ryan either. Every time he goes into his garage he sees sacks of mail waiting to be answered. They are arriving at the rate of two big Post Office bags a week – I think there were seven before the season had even kicked off. His grandad used to look after the fan mail. He is retired and I think he enjoyed helping Ryan answer the queries and organise photographs and autographs, but he has no chance of catching up. I think the situation upsets Ryan because he doesn't like letting people down, but what can he do?

I first noticed this tremendous surge of popularity at the Cliff training ground. Fans have been going there for years to watch the training and ask for autographs as we leave. The majority have been young lads interested in football, often there with their mums and dads, perhaps in the school holidays. Lately, though, the girls have been coming in groups of seven or eight and only want to see Giggsy or Lee Sharpe. I don't think they even go to matches; they just want to get near him, and they now outnumber the boys. You always know if it's Giggsy leaving the training ground by the volume of noise and the high-pitched screaming!

He has a great talent and everything seems to have snow-balled in the last few months. Television has latched on to him as someone special, which means that he has become a per-sonality projected instantly into the nation's living-rooms. I see the same thing happening when we are away with the Wales team. Kevin Ratcliffe has won around 70 international caps for Wales and you wouldn't think he would be easily impressed by anyone or anything concerning football. He has been everywhere and rubbed shoulders with the great names of the game, but when Giggs made his début for us against Belgium all Rats could says afterwards was, well, at least I can tell my kids that I have played with Ryan Giggs.

It's all heady, mind-boggling stuff and inevitably you worry if it is going to spoil Giggsy and see him get carried away. Hopefully, he won't let it turn his head – in fact, I think he knows that basically everything starts and finishes with what he does on the pitch. If he forgets that fundamental truth, he is finished because you only play for a club like Manchester United if you deliver. I don't really have any fears for him because he has his head screwed on right and he always has the manager and his team-mates to make sure he keeps everything in perspective. A dressing-room, with its banter and plenty of stick flying around, is a minefield for anyone getting too big for their boots and Giggsy gets plenty of teasing. He has a good sense of humour and he can see the funny side so I can't see him changing. He is young and I suppose he is not bad looking if you like that sort of thing, so he might as well make the most of it while it lasts because soon he will be as old as Brucey and able to answer all his fan mail in ten minutes!

As far as the other players are concerned, what really counts is the football he contributes out on the park, and we can certainly have no complaint about either the effort or skill he puts into every match. He must have found his first season in the senior side as frustrating as the rest of us. As a young player, the manager had nursed him through the traumatic season which had seen Leeds come from behind to snatch the title from us. He occasionally left him out of the side so that he wouldn't burn out early. The boss kept insisting that he wanted Ryan to be a star at 27 as well as 17, but naturally we had all noted his gifts in that first season and his arrival in the big-time was one of the factors that lifted us as we prepared to try again in season 1992–93.

Obviously, we all felt pretty low at getting so near to the Championship after so long striving to win it. I think quite a few people wondered if there was a curse on the club in terms of the League title. The wheel had wobbled and the big question was whether it would now fall off. I'm sure that was the worry passing through the minds of the supporters as they waited for the new season. In the dressing-room we quickly got our minds round the issue and I think there was a quiet resolve that this time we would do it, no matter what. The manager told us that sometimes you have to suffer pain before you can enjoy the sweet fruits of success. Well, we had certainly had a bellyful of pain and no one wanted that again. We examined all the reasons for our failure. It wasn't a matter of looking for excuses but to understand where we had gone wrong and what could be done to improve our challenge.

We knew we had had injuries and had finished with too much on our plate, but that wouldn't necessarily repeat itself. We reminded ourselves that it hadn't all been bad. We had won the Rumbelows Cup and even if we had not finished first in the League, we had still proved ourselves better than 20 other clubs. Runners-up isn't exactly failure and we came to the conclusion that we would make sure that the experience would only serve to make us stronger.

Above all, we vowed that the cynics who said we would never do it, that we were fated never to win the Championship and that we would always crack as the pressure built up, would simply be used as a spur to stiffen us. We had confidence in ourselves and we were determined to prove it. The manager did his stuff by signing Dion Dublin to give us another option in attack, and, as I say, we all realised that Giggsy would be stronger and really ready to fly.

We were not wrong either. He spread his wings and had a marvellous season, producing some devastating work on the wing, not only creating chances with his crosses but scoring himself to finish second highest scorer with 11 goals in all competitions, two more than Brian McClair and Eric Cantona. I was pleased with my goal tally of 16, with 15 of them in the League, as we steamed through an exhilarating season to bring the Championship to Old Trafford for the first time since Sir Matt Busby had won it in 1967.

I can't begin to describe to you the joy and satisfaction when we finally emerged League winners and rode through Manchester in an open-top bus, surrounded by delighted and appreciative supporters. We have capped that success by following with a League and Cup double, but, for me at any rate, this was the season which meant the most, the big break-through, the trophy which after 26 long, tortuous years finally said we were the best.

Perhaps the longer-serving players felt it the most, because when you had been at Old Trafford for a little while you felt you were carrying the burden of the whole 26 years and that it was your fault the fans had had to wait so long for this particular trophy. I know it's nonsense to blame present players for the failures of the past, but that's what it felt like and it's a heavy load. The relief when we crossed the finishing line first was something special. The tension had become almost unbearable and though we have done well since I believe it has been mainly because we had got the monkey off our backs, enabling us to play as free spirits.

This was the season that did it, though it didn't feel that way when we opened the campaign with two defeats to arouse all the fears and frustrations of the previous year. It seemed fate was still against us in the shape of Brian Hill, who is not Manchester United's favourite referee, and sure enough the result at Sheffield United hinged on penalty situations. We were in trouble as early as the fifth minute, when Brian Deane scored. We thought we had the chance to equalise quarter of an hour later but Mr Hill saw nothing wrong when their goal-keeper brought down Giggsy in an incident described later on radio by Tommy Docherty as a penalty 'a million times over'.

Then in the second half, to add insult to injury, Sheffield were awarded a penalty, which was converted by Deane. I pulled a goal back but we couldn't add to it and had to come home with a 2–1 defeat.

We fared even worse four days later, going down at home 3–0 to Everton. This was definitely not what the fans expected, nor us for that matter. As usual, I found Neville Southall difficult to beat and he made one particularly good save from me. For long spells we played quite well, with our wingers busy, but I'm afraid to say the lads at the back didn't have their customary grip and Everton seemed to score on nearly every breakaway. So there we were, the Championship hopefuls, dumped at the bottom of the table, even though we hadn't had much luck going for us.

Perhaps we were still mentally on our holidays, and though we stopped the losing rot against Ipswich in the next match, and Denis Irwin's goal was a belter, a 1–1 draw at home was not quite what we wanted. Ipswich have become a tough team for us, hard to break down when they employ their negative tactics aimed simply at stopping us scoring. In fairness, they do defend well, with John Wark a brilliant organiser at the back. Nevertheless, it was a grim situation when we set off for Southampton looking for our first win after three games without one. The position looked even blacker when we still hadn't scored with just a minute remaining. It was the moment Dion dashed to the rescue to mark his full début with a very valuable goal for a 1–0 victory. Who knows, without that win we might never have gone on to win the Championship. There was a long way to go but if we hadn't managed a win in that game we might have gone to pieces. As it was, we seemed inspired and reeled off five straight wins to launch our challenge in a bold, dominant fashion.

We went to Nottingham Forest and the buzz was back in the side as Giggsy and I scored in a solid 2–0 win. I was on the scoresheet in the next game, scoring a typical poacher's goal for a 1-0 at home to Crystal Palace. Unfortunately, it wasn't such a good day for poor old Dion, who had to be stretchered off with a shattered ankle. He had shown for a ball from the back and virtually had it when Eric Young moved in to nick it away from him. He caught him on the ankle, a pure accident, and with Dion also twisting it as he fell, he was left with not just a broken bone but badly torn ligaments as well. It was nearly the end of the season before he was playing again.

He stayed amazingly cheerful during the time he spent recovering from the injury. He is a great bloke and very popular in the dressing-room. His chances have been limited but he doesn't complain. In fact, he just seems happy to be part of the United set-up. I think he loves the place and I am sure his time will come. For such a tall man he has a good touch and knows a few tricks. Old Trafford has not seen the best of him yet.

Anyway, with the help of his winning goal at the Dell we were now on a winning streak with a full head of steam up. Goals from Brucey and Andrei saw us beat Leeds at Old Trafford for a very satisfying 2-0 victory. It was an important performance because it showed that we were perfectly capable of matching the reigning champions. We felt we had a point to prove because, in our minds, we had been the best team the previous season but had finished without the right trophy to prove it. It was a big game and I should have done more myself to make sure Leeds realised we meant business. I failed in a one-on-one with the goalkeeper and I had also hit the post, but Andrei with a rare header and a typical Bruce tap-in gave us victory and boosted our confidence that this time we could go one better than Elland Road.

Critics maintained that the weakness of our challenge the previous season had been our failure to beat any of the major teams, and two draws with Leeds, the eventual champions, had underlined the point. So this was an important win for us. It was a convincing performance and we had clawed our way back up the table. Norwich were the early pace-setters but we were now in fourth place, just three points behind the leaders. We produced another solid performance in the next game to win 2–0 at Everton and compensate for the early season defeat against the Goodison Park club. Choccy and Steve, with a penalty, were our goal-scorers.

Events proved the importance of that five-match winning burst because we then entered a month or so of drawn games which saw us treading water in the League and crashing out of two Cup competitions. We lost on penalties against Torpedo Moscow in the UEFA Cup after drawing goalless at both Old Trafford and in Russia. We even drew against Brighton before winning the second leg, 1–0, in the Coca-Cola Cup. We went out of this competition as well in the next round, losing 1–0 at Aston Villa. We missed a lot of chances and I was one of the culprits. Clayton got some stick as well. He was chatting to our Welsh team-mate, Dean Saunders, at the near post when Deano suddenly left him, got the ball and scored. He really caught a blast from the defenders for that one.

Overall, though, it was the low scoring which was our undoing and which also saw us limping along in the League. I suppose 1–1 at Spurs wasn't too bad but we should have done better than 0–0 against QPR on our own ground. Everything seemed to be going wrong for us at Old Trafford at this stage and the fact that the Stretford End had been pulled down for redevelopment work gave the stadium an eerie atmosphere. It seemed odd to be playing without the most vocal section of the ground in full cry. Arsenal put a plywood screen with a rent-a-crowd painted on it when they rebuilt the North Bank, which indicates how much importance they attached to the support from their home terracing. But, even though we didn't have the Stretford Enders roaring us on, we salvaged some pride when we pulled back from two goals down to draw 2–2 against the old enemy from Anfield. Liverpool were good value for their lead and there were only ten minutes to go when I helped a chip from Clayton past Bruce Grobbelaar and then a minute before time scored when Giggsy whipped the ball back to me.

The fight-back should have done us a power of good but we were back to a goalless game at Blackburn and then three successive defeats. We lost our Coca-Cola Cup tie at Villa, crashed to a home defeat against the crazy gang from Wimbledon and then went down to Villa again in the League. Dalian Atkinson did the damage and but for Peter Schmeichel we might have been on the receiving end of a real drubbing. The defeat meant that, taking all competitions into account, we had won only one of our last 12 games. Our scoring had dried up and we had slipped back to tenth in the table. The manager began talking openly about reinforcements, and, indeed, it was at this stage of the season that he made his move for Eric Cantona.

He had bought Dion and then lost him through injury, which had put the squad back to square one. Something was clearly missing in terms of making a sustained Championship challenge. At the beginning of November we did, in fact, get Lee Sharpe back in action after his saga of injuries and illness. His first game of the season was the League defeat at Villa Park but his return gave the boss another option and he helped us bounce back with a 3–0 home win against Oldham and a 1–0 win at Arsenal. Despite those two wins, though, the boss had decided that we needed a boost and his answer was Eric Cantona. Little did we know at the time the extent of the boost, one which in fact would transform the whole situation.

Eric made his début in a red shirt by coming on for the second half of the Old Trafford derby. I think he contented himself with just trotting around and getting to know us. Perhaps just his presence gave us a lift because he inspired Incey to score his first goal of the season and, with one from me, we sent City away with a 2–1 defeat. We marked Eric's full début with a 1–0 win against Norwich at home. I got the goal and maintained my scoring form to make it a run of four goals in four games. We had to be content with a 1–1 draw at Chelsea but on a ground which had previously proved tricky for us it wasn't a bad result. Eric got the goal, his first of many for United, and I was really enjoying the partnership. His arrival proved the missing link. The team felt right, balanced and we were creating chances. The improvement up front also saw a tightening up at the back and confidence flooded through the team. Slowly but surely, the feeling gripped the team that no matter how a game seemed to be going against us we were capable of pulling something out of the bag. We began to establish a reputation for not knowing when we were beaten, and there was no better illustration of our refusal to accept defeat than the Boxing Day match against Sheffield Wednesday at Hillsborough.

David Hirst, the striker the boss had tried unsuccessfully to buy, scored after only three minutes and after an hour's play we were three goals down. Even the most fanatical of our fans had given up at that point, but Sharpey went mad to provide a stream of crosses which led to two goals from Choccy McClair and an equaliser from Eric for a 3–3 draw. By the end we had Wednesday on the ropes, praying for the final whistle. We just never gave up, that was the big difference in the side, and we went to town a couple of days later by beating Coventry 5–0 at Old Trafford. Eric and I both scored, along with Sharpey, Giggsy and Denis Irwin.

The scoring famine was behind us and we really began to strike terror into the opposition. Very often, if Eric didn't score I did and lots of the others were joining in. We put four past Spurs and scored three against QPR. We lost at Ipswich but beat Forest and Sheffield United to go to the top of the table again. We could only draw 0–0 at Leeds but under the circumstances it was a very good result. The papers often talk in exaggerated terms about certain grounds being a cauldron of hate but Elland Road on this occasion was a really mean place. You could feel the hostility seething round the ground, not among the players I might add, but from the Leeds fans, who seemed to have taken the transfer of Eric as a personal insult.

Clearly, they regarded him as a traitor and they were out to show that they hated him. It was all very unfair because, after all, he had helped them win the Championship in 1992 for the first time in 18 years, not quite as big a gap as Manchester United had experienced but I would have thought it had been long enough to have made the Leeds supporters a little more appreciative of the players who had returned the glory years. It's their business, but their treatment of Eric was scandalous for his first return following his transfer.

It was hardly surprising that under this torrent of abuse something snapped in Eric as he left the field and he got involved with a Leeds supporter, which later saw him in trouble with the FA. It's very easy to preach about good behaviour but you must take provocation into account before condemning anyone and I must say that during the match the conduct of the players was impeccable. That's the curious thing about the relationship between Leeds and Manchester United. Terrible words, like scum, fly about in the fanzines when the extremists among the fans refer to their rivals but as far as the players are concerned we all get on very well. You couldn't possibly dislike someone like Gordon Strachan, and their captain, Gary McAllister, came over for Sir Matt Busby's funeral last season, which tells you something about the respect we hold for each other. This particular game was highly competitive but there was nothing nasty or vicious out on the pitch and I find it sad that the fans don't get on better.

Anyway, our away point kept us on top, though it was probably the result of the next match which did more to see us through to the Championship because it saw us knocked out of the FA Cup, the final distraction. We were now out of everything – the Rumbelows Cup, Europe and finally the FA Cup – to leave us free to concentrate on the League without any fixture congestion or thoughts of Wembley to complicate our effort. Last season, of course, we took everything in our stride, League and Cup, but the ability to fire on all fronts successfully comes with success and confidence. In the season under review here, you have to remember that we were fresh from the disappointment of seeing the Championship slip through our fingers the previous year and I think players and fans alike all had it in their minds that we might crack up again.

Certainly, there was disappointment in the dressing-room after losing 2–1 to Sheffield United at Bramall Lane in the Cup fifth round. We have often found the Blades difficult to handle and we certainly did in this match. Giggsy gave us a good start with a goal after half an hour but Jamie Hoyland, who comes from Manchester, took just three minutes to equalise and by half-time they had gone ahead. I thought we would get a replay out of it when we got a penalty six minutes from the end. Eric wasn't playing that day and Brucey took over again as our penalty-taker. It didn't look right, with the ball not properly on the spot and a Sheffield player encroaching in the box to point it out, but Steve carried on and hit the post. He had done brilliantly for us in the past with penalties and we had to swallow our disappointment. No one blamed him, except perhaps his little boy, who we learned later had greeted his father at the front door with those immortal words: 'Dad, what were you doing?'

My eldest, Alex, was at the Bobby Charlton soccer school this summer and is increasingly aware of what goes on in football and Manchester United. I guess one day, just as I think I have escaped from the frantic world of winning and losing into the peace and quiet of my own home, I am going to get hit between the eyes with that kind of question about some open goal I have missed. I'm not sure at the moment how I will be able to react!

Anyway, thanks to Steve's penalty miss we had been left with a nicely spaced League programme and just one thought in our minds: to make sure that we clinched the long-awaited League title. As the record shows, we did indeed get the bit between our teeth. Of the remaining 14 games we won ten, drew three and lost only one. It was a blistering finish, even if I say so myself, and it burned off Aston Villa to see us win the Premiership by ten points. We bounced back from the Cup defeat to beat Southampton 2–1 at Old Trafford. Mind you, we had a bit of a fright after substitute Nicky Banger had given the Saints the lead with only quarter of an hour to go. It was Giggsy who saved the day for us with two beautiful goals in the last ten minutes and the kind of performance which launched him into the frenzied orbit I described at the beginning of the chapter. We owed him a lot in that game because up front neither Eric nor I had done much and we certainly needed a win to reinforce our mood that we could go all the way for the title.

We were much more convincing in the next game, with a 3–0 win at home against Middlesbrough. There was more magic from Ryan but it was Denis Irwin we all felt delighted for as he marked his 100th League appearance for the Reds with a goal scored with one of his excellently struck free kicks. Eric dropped out for the next two games with suspension and in the first 20 minutes at Liverpool there was certainly something missing in our play. We took a fearful hammering but with our newly acquired resilience we stood the game on its head. I scored just before the interval and Liverpool must have gone off wondering how they could possibly be behind. Ian Rush equalised but again we came back and Choccy scored the winner. Big Pete in goal, though, was the star man when things were running against us and one save in particular from Don Hutchison was out of this world.

We had a hiccup away to Oldham, who were fighting for their lives against relegation. Bottom beat top 1–0 and it was a reminder that there is many a slip 'twixt cup and lip, but perhaps it put us on our mettle for the following game, which was a vital top-of-the-table clash. We were at home to Villa, the team chasing us to the finishing line, and obviously the result was of extreme importance to both teams. Steve Staunton put Villa ahead with a great shot, and I thought, here we go again, but just eight minutes later a cross from Denis was pushed back across goal for me to head in. Another Cantona-Hughes one-two and we had succeeded in holding Villa at bay.

The form book goes out of the window for a derby match and we had to be content with 1–1 at Maine Road. Slightly more worrying was a goalless result at Arsenal, our third draw in a row on top of a defeat, a spell which had seen us score just two goals in four games. It was hardly title form and, inevitably, people were beginning to ask if our nerves were raw again and wonder whether we were starting to twitch. I remember saying at the time, though, that there were no alarm bells ringing in the dressing-room because there was one very big difference compared with the previous season's slip-up. This time, although our scoring rate had slumped, we were still creating chances and we were all confident that our luck would change and that we would soon hit the goal trail again.

My confidence was soon proved justified because we promptly reeled off a super seven straight wins to see off our rivals. The first one was at Norwich, which I missed through suspension. The boss could have played safe and put Robbo in but he boldly went out to maintain our attacking force and selected Andrei instead. It paid off, with a great 3–1 win, an important result which put us back in the frame after slipping out of it. We were now second in the table, just one point behind Villa and with a better goal difference. We played some marvellous football and all three goals, from Andrei, Giggsy and Eric, came in a blitz of eight minutes. The next game was the one which told us we were destined to win the Championship. Sheffield Wednesday were leading 1–0 at Old Trafford with only four minutes to go, though in actual fact there was longer because of injury time. Nevertheless, there didn't seem enough to pull this one out of the fire until old Roy of the Rovers got busy and the incredible Steve Bruce gave us a 2–1 victory with a couple of headers. His first was from an Irwin corner and the other came from Pally. The fact that both central defenders were up in the opposing penalty box shows we were a bit gung-ho for a win.

Easter clinched it for us, with a narrow one-goal win through a Denis Irwin rocket at Coventry, followed by an easy 3–0 win at home to Chelsea, when their goalkeeper had an off-day, and a decisive 2–0 success at Crystal Palace. Villa had kicked off earlier than us that day and we knew they were three down at half-time. What an incentive that was, and I was a particularly happy man when I scored to give me a hundred League goals for United. Our fans finished the match chanting: 'We're going to win the League', and they were spot on. Villa lost 1–0 at home to Oldham on the Sunday to make us champions without kicking another ball.

A lot of people said they would have liked us to have won it out on the pitch playing in a match, and I understand what they mean, but I have got to say it was very special for me to become a champion in my own home surrounded by the people closest to me. The boss told us we shouldn't watch the Villa game on television and I think he went for a game of golf with his eldest son. I must admit I was nervous, and drifted in and out of the living-room. I spent a lot of time in the kitchen making cups of tea and then we all came back in front of the television for the last five minutes. I told the kids that in a few minutes I might be giving them the biggest hugs they had ever had in their lives. I don't think they really understood but they knew something special was in the air and when the final whistle went for Oldham's victory we were all in tears, me especially. The Welsh are very emotional, you know!

Later on I went round to Steve Bruce's house to find most of the other players there and we had rather a wild party. In fact, to be honest I don't really know how we managed to get through the game against Blackburn at Old Trafford a couple of days later, let alone win 3–1. The match was remarkable in many ways, not just for the fact that Manchester United were champions after 26 long painful years but because Gary Pallister scored his first and only goal of the season. It was a super night all round and it was more than obvious that the fans loved every minute of it. They gave us a tremendous reception and I felt that while everyone was clearly happy and excited there was a particular heartfelt message of appreciation coming across from older fans who could perhaps remember the great glory years of Sir Matt Busby. I know that once we had had time to reflect on the significance of our Championship win that we all felt moved by the fact that we had finally done it in Sir Matt's lifetime. I think one of the most important memories will be of the way Sir Matt stood smiling in the directors' box when we went up for our medals and the trophy was lifted jointly by Robbo and Steve Bruce.

It was a great night and one I was delighted to share with the fans, who over the years have been very kind to me and who gave us great support in the anxious days leading up to the Championship crunch. We went down to Wimbledon for the final game of the season and another party. We even signed off in style with another win and we managed to get Robbo on the scoresheet for his first and only League goal of the season. It was also great timing that we had at last pulled in the Championship for Robbo after his magnificent service at Old Trafford. It was a perfect finish to a perfect season, and even though we enjoyed the heady delights of a League and

FA Cup double last year, that first Championship since 1967 will remain very special and precious to everyone who helped bring it back to Old Trafford.

I think time will tell that it was a highly significant break-through and there were some very handsome tributes from the United players who had last won the League. George Best, for instance, said: 'I cannot pay a bigger compliment than to say that the present team stands comparison with the great side I played in which won the First Division title in 1967 and the European Cup the following year. In my time, if the team had an off-day, we could always rely on one of the players to produce something a little bit special, and this is one of the secrets of Alex Ferguson's team.'

A particular hero of mine, Denis Law, probably because like me he played at the sharp end, summed up a lot of people's feelings when he said: 'When the Reds slipped up over the last leg of the previous season I began to wonder if the title was ever coming back to Old Trafford. But the team have made it this season, and made it in style.'

I also enjoyed the words of Kenny Dalglish, so long a rival at Liverpool and now taking Blackburn to great things. Like the down-to-earth professional that he is, he posed the next challenge when he said: 'United proved they are fitting champions and have set a standard which the rest of us must match. Only time will tell what heights Manchester United will reach from now on because you can never be sure how players will react to success.'

Well, I think we have made a good start towards answering his question. We didn't sit back and say to ourselves that's enough. We didn't go soft and allow ourselves to be swept away on a tide of adulation. We won the Championship again and we landed the rare League and FA Cup double for the first time in United's history. There is still more to achieve, such as the European Cup, and it would certainly be satisfying to become only the second club after Liverpool since the last world war to win a third successive Championship.

It's a tall order but so was what we have achieved in the last couple of seasons and you can take it from me that the mood at Manchester United is that we haven't finished yet!

Chapter Eleven

DUKE OF MOTTRAM

THE lads call me the Duke of Mottram these days. It's their way of having a dig at my lifestyle as a family man with three children, complete with accessories like a Range Rover and Alsatian dog. I'm also having a house built in Mottram St Andrew, close to where I live at present, which no doubt helps my team-mates to see me as an aspiring country squire. All I need now are the green wellies! It's good for a laugh, and if you can't take a joke in a football dressing-room, you are dead. Part of the jibe is true anyway, because I am putting roots down. I said at the outset of this book that I wanted to finish my career with Manchester United and, while it's difficult to predict the future in this game, it's still my aim.

Things can change very quickly of course. When I was writing the first chapter there was a distinct possibility that Chris Sutton would come to Old Trafford. Now, as I pen the final piece, he's a Blackburn player. It was always a situation that could affect my future. United have, in fact, offered me a new contract to replace my present agreement, which has got just one year to run. It was a bit on the short side for my liking at first. I'm 30 now and the club were obviously keeping their options open in case another Sutton comes along. I pressed them for a longer deal and hopefully we have now reached agreement. I believe I have another five years as a top player and I want those final seasons to be at Old Trafford. I don't see myself going down the divisions. I'm in a fortunate position financially so that I won't have to spin my career out longer than I feel I can cope with. I consider that a lot of the problems such as arthritis faced by former professionals in later life stem from pushing themselves for too long and playing with knocks that should be rested at an age when injuries take longer to mend.

Will I stay in the game as a manager or coach? I love the game and if I had not been a professional I would have played for fun but, at the moment, I can't see myself going into management. I'm not a football fanatic. The players who stay in the game are usually those who want to watch every fixture shown on television and go to matches at all levels. I'm afraid I don't eat, sleep and live football. I don't go along with the Bill Shankly philosophy that football is not a matter of life and death, it's more important. I find I have other things to do, as anyone with three children would understand. Alex, who is six, Curtis aged four and Xenna coming up two fill a large part of my spare time. I enjoy being involved with them and I also have my golf. I'm even learning to play the piano.

Peter Schmeichel, who I told you earlier is a very good pianist himself, got me interested. I started off asking his advice on buying a piano as a piece of furniture and for the kids to learn on but now I'm having lessons myself. You might think it doesn't quite fit the image of a fiery Red Dragon, but it's really a matter of the wheel turning full circle. As a boy, I was taught the violin and played in the school orchestra. I only gave it up because I felt like a cissy carrying a violin case on the bus. I had a musical bent as a kid and my old primary-

179

school teacher in Ruabon used to like to tell people he had a cassette of a lovely treble voice singing *O Little Town of Bethlehem* at a Christmas carol service. Yes, folks, it was me. I'm not so worried about what people think these days and I don't think too many see me as a cissy!

Perhaps when all my children are in school I'll see things differently about staying in the game. I may have ideas and feel I want to try them out. We'll see when the time comes. Meanwhile, there is more to achieve as a player, and not just with Manchester United. I take my international career with Wales very seriously and I'm looking forward to working with our new team boss, Mike Smith. Actually, I got off to a bad start following his appointment and his announcement that I was in his first squad to go to Estonia for a friendly at the end of last season. I was unfit, having suffered a recurrence of my heel injury, only Alex Ferguson forgot to tell him and, apparently, there were a few awkward questions from the press when I failed to appear as expected. It's all sorted out now but it wasn't the best of starts and I hope he doesn't let it change his mind after telling me that I could play up front again with Ian Rush. Naturally, I am prepared to play in any position asked of me for Wales but striker is definitely my best role and I'm looking forward to resuming a partnership which was very successful at the start of my international career.

Perhaps we may have Juventus chasing us again. For just before I returned to United in 1988, the Italian club watched us play together for Wales. They already had Rushie and I'm told they fancied the idea of pairing us up together after we had played against Italy and won. I got word of their interest just a few days after signing for United so they were too late. I understand they even offered United a profit on what they had just paid Barcelona but there was nothing doing.

My first manager with Wales was Mike England, a great player who unfortunately didn't win anything much as a manager, although he did establish himself as one of the best-loved bosses in the game. He inspired great loyalty and I think the politics of Welsh football, with the rivalry between north and south, brought his reign to a halt sooner than it should. He was a classic victim of Welsh FA wrangling. I was sorry to see him go, though happily for Wales he was succeeded by Terry Yorath, a guy who also engendered a terrific spirit among the players. It took time to build up, though, and he went before he had the opportunity to cash in on his efforts. John Toshack took over but after only one game in charge he went back to Spain. He had a look and clearly didn't like what he saw.

Mike Smith has had an involvement with Welsh football at youth level for a long time and I'm sure his policy now will be to bring through a lot of promising youngsters with Welsh credentials who are around in the game. I just hope he is given time to get established. In my view, a young player needs ten or 15 caps to get to grips with the game at international level. Some see Wales as a ragbag team but, with a bit of luck, I think we could be knocked into shape to produce something useful. Maybe we could create more of a team identity if we all started to speak Welsh! I'm afraid I would have a bit to do because although English was a second language to my grandmother, I only got to CSE level in Welsh. In fact, there are only two Welsh regulars who are fluent – Malcolm Allen of Newcastle and Leicester's Ewan Roberts. Seriously, though, we have been very close to success several times and with patience and perhaps a touch more luck we'll do something really good before I have to hang up my boots.

We have some sparkling individuals, not least our own Giggsy, who we sometimes call Robin after the Boy Wonder but who is more often known simply as George. Well, everyone else compares him with George Best and all players detest being called the second anyone so that's why Ryan gets George. Although he grew up in Salford and captained the England schoolboy team, I know he has a great fondness and loyalty to Wales. With him in our side we could go places and hopefully in return give him a deserved World Cup platform one day. I was very encouraged during the summer to read that he felt the older Welsh players still had enough left in them to make up for past disappointments. Thanks, George, I'll do my best, I assure you!

If we could develop the same sort of image as the Scots or the Irish, maybe the media would take us more seriously. As I discovered to my cost in Barcelona, the press can do you a lot of good but can also make life very difficult for you. Overall, I cannot complain about the treatment I have had from the media, at least in this country. At the time of my testimonial the papers said a lot of kind things about my career, so generous that I thought I would let them have the last word in my book! The newspaper boys usually do anyway and so I shall let them blow my trumpet for me with their testimonial tributes. These are the favourite bits from my scrapbook!

Peter Ball of the *Times*

'People often say about Mark that he is a scorer of great goals rather than a great goalscorer. Half of that is right. Ever since he first came into United's side, he has scored goals which just take the breath away. I remember two volleys against Aston Villa the day before he won the Young Player of the Year award in 1985. One was a goal – the more breathtaking almost shattered the post. That power and timing has never left him. I don't think I've ever seen a harder shot than the goal against Southampton last season. But his goalscoring record, for a player who has developed into an outstanding leader of the line, is not half bad – nearly one every two games before going to Barcelona and better than one in three since his return. But what that equation ignores is his ability for scoring vital goals. Has there ever been a more crucial one than his equaliser in the semi-final against Oldham which revived United's season? Well, there were the two against Crystal Palace at Wembley and the two against Barcelona. When the chips are down, Sparky is your man. He will go down as one of United's greatest forwards and there is no higher praise.'

Guy Hodgson of the *Independent*

'My lingering memory of Mark Hughes will not be the spectacular goals, although there have been some that you would have presumed could exist in only the richest fantasies, but his ability to make time seemingly stand still. A pass will be played into the hurly-burly of the most congested area of the pitch and suddenly everything around him appears to freeze. He will make to go one way, dummy to pass the other, all the time defenders mesmerised by the brooding figure in the blood-red shirt. It makes him unique, the only person going at natural speed while everyone else is in a slow-motion replay. Defenders loathe to mark him, opposition supporters give him the compliment of simply loathing him (while secretly wishing he was wearing their colours). For if Mark Hughes has been anything in his 12 years at United it has been the standard-bearer for the common fan. No matter how poor the team's performance, the Stretford Ender has known that Sparky has tried his heart out. Now it is the time for Old Trafford to say thank you.'

David Walker of the *Daily Mail*

'In the immediate aftermath to disappointing results by British club and international teams, Jimmy Hill and his band of professional pundits invariably denounce the lack of skill and technique among our footballers these days. They dare not table that particular slur in Mark Hughes's direction. Perhaps he is a throw-back to another generation. In fact, I suspect Sparky would have been a truly outstanding striker in any era of the game because there are two great ingredients to his approach. The first is the god-given talent to strike a ball so sweetly with either foot, allied to the exquisite balance that helps him pass with poise and instinctive direction. The second is a bravery and competitive instinct that has under-standably seen him win the acclaim of United's fans. I recall from my own youth idolising not just the great players, but especially those who played with passion for their team. The men who stood up to aggressors and refused to back down. Alongside the likes of Steve Bruce and Paul Ince, Mark has provided the vital competitive edge that has been critical to United successfully defending their Premiership crown. I believe his testimonial game is being played at the climax to the finest season of Mark's career. He is a team man and a vital ingredient of a great team. But to United fans he will go down in history alongside the likes of Denis Law, Bryan Robson and Nobby Stiles as one of the players who gave their all for the Red cause and always stood up to be counted.'

Derek Potter, formerly of the *Daily Express*

'Instinct and timing made Jimmy Greaves a sneak-thief in the penalty box. Razor-sharp reactions and bravery were the qualities that brought Denis "The Demon" Law so many glorious goals. With other leading strikers, quality in the air has been the key to unlock defences. Mark Hughes scores his goals with a combination of all the talents of the pastmasters. Then there is his personal hallmark of power. Though two inches short of six feet, Mark has often outjumped giant defenders to head memorable goals. Who would deny that his last-gasp equaliser against Oldham Athletic at Wembley was as lethal as Law at his best? That goal may have salvaged United's season and doomed Oldham. And to complete the generation picture, many old-timers will think of Bobby Charlton and Jack Rowley when they watch Hughes drill the goals in from long range. Definitely a man to be feared and respected in the goal zone.'

Ken Lawrence of the *Daily Mirror*

'Mark Hughes may not thank me for this because it might just spoil his macho-man image, but deep down he's really just a big softie! His cover was blown a few months ago when he became involved in Operation Christmas Child, a relief agency formed to help the starving, sick or disabled children of war-torn Bosnia. Sparky, a big family man himself, was shown around OCC's Wrexham centre of operations where food, clothes, blankets and tiny coffins were stored before being airlifted out. He took home books and videos which revealed the true horror of what was happening in the former Yugoslavia. I know what he heard, read and saw upset him a lot. But that's Sparky for you. On the pitch as hard as they come, a true leader of Old Trafford. Off it, he has a completely different persona. Talk about not taking your work home with you. So the next time you see Sparky give his all in another of those famous, red-blooded challenges of his, remember that he's got a big heart in more ways than one. Congratulations, Sparky and good luck.'

Peter Fitton of the *Sun*

'It's an admission explosive enough to provoke a civil war in football, but the man who saved Mark Hughes's seriously threatened career was a Leeds United fan. Sid Owen was his

name and he played an influential role in the creation of Don
Revie's powerful empire at Elland Road in the Sixties and
. Seventies. By the time he trekked across the Pennines to enlist
as a coach in Dave Sexton's Old Trafford camp, Sparky was
just about arriving on the scene. Soon he was in big trouble.
Homesick for his Welsh pals in Ruabon and desperate at his
failure to make any impact in United's junior ranks, only the
dole queue seemed to be looming for the teenage Hughes.
Then Sid, a man who had helped shape the impressive careers
of Billy Bremner, Johnny Giles and Norman Hunter, had a
brainwave. Sparky was shunted from midfield to striker. Since
that decision of destiny, he has told me often enough: "Sid
only did that because I couldn't get a game anywhere else –
and that was in the A team! Honestly, I was going nowhere."
The rest is history with Hughes, in a dozen years of glory,
turning himself into one of the greatest front-liners United
have ever hired. He has proved himself so often the physical
sacrifice to the cause, a big-match saviour and a footballer
blessed with fans from both the dressing-room and on the ter-
races. There can't be a greater tribute.'

Paul Walker of the *Daily Star*

'Steve Bruce summed Mark Hughes up recently when he
said: "Thank God I don't have to face him on the pitch."
United's skipper is the only centre-half in the land who has
the luxury of watching Hughes in action – from a safe distance! Because in five years of marvellous success at Old
Trafford it is Sparky who has led the line, it's Sparky who
scores the vital goals in the big, big matches and it's Sparky
who never hides when the going gets tough. United's style
with Eric Cantona having a free role and two wide men on
the flanks means it's Sparky who has to take the brunt of the
physical stuff from opposing defenders. He always shows for

the ball, and that's what makes him so special. Without the focal point of their attacks, Cantona would not have the space he needs to cause havoc and the wingers would be denied the right service. Hughes has taken it and dished it out with barely a murmur for seasons and United's fans appreciate exactly what he's done for the club and how vital he is to the team. And, of course, there are those big-game goals. The equaliser against Palace in the 1990 Cup final rescued the side that day. The "double" in the European Cup Winners Cup final. The last-ditch equaliser at Wembley against Oldham this season. It's Sparky to be relied upon when it matters. It's been a pleasure watching him, not so much of a pleasure when you have to play against him. Brucey, you're a lucky man.'

John Bean of the *Daily Express*

'The Welshman they call "Thunder Thighs" played the violin as a schoolboy until he decided that carrying the case on the school bus made him look cissy. Since those days Mark Hughes has been more intent on creating crashing football cadenzas for Manchester United. This season they have never sounded better. Ten years after his league début for United in March 1984, Mark has discovered a rare harmony with Eric Cantona. For manager Alex Ferguson, the marriage of Hughes's skill, strength and aggression at the painful end of United's operation with Cantona's subtle, dynamic work is made in heaven. It didn't happen easily. Mark's highly individual style up front – no one controls or shields the ball better – baffled a series of United partners from Frank Stapleton to Brian McClair. It is Sparky's good fortune that in his late 20s he should find Cantona – but no more than this truly great United pro deserves. Rake through the embers of 1993–94 season and you will see the glow of some of the best goals Hughes has ever scored. The pick of them? Well, the thunderous last-minute FA Cup semi-final equaliser against Oldham takes some beating. It was the 19th strike of his season and effectively kept United's campaign alive and kicking. But the 20th, in the penultimate game against Southampton, was just as good. It's been that sort of season for Mark Hughes. No one deserves tonight's tribute more.'

David Maddock of *Today*

'Mark Hughes is undoubtedly a fine player, but perhaps more importantly, in the great scheme of things, he is a fine man. Forget all about that posturing, bluff approach on the pitch. Away from football, as I'm sure many Manchester United fans are aware, he is a softly spoken, almost shy character. He is also a thoroughly likeable man who is generous with his time and patient in attitude – which sets him apart from many of the so-called superstars of the modern game. Mark is aware of the responsibility of his position in the public eye and, like his colleague Bryan Robson, donates a lot of time and energy to worthwhile causes; notably helping orphaned youngsters recently. Let's not overlook that impressive, swashbuckling figure he cuts in action, however. Like an epic thirties film star he excites passion in the adoring Old Trafford faithful as he slides through opposing defences. His aggression is not an image though, but a product of his professionalism, because Mark knows it is only his desire and commitment which allow him to continue to flourish at the peak of a ruthlessly competitive sport. It is that dedication which has seen him play such a vital part this season as the Reds gallantly retained their title. Indeed, many people, myself among them, would say his role was the decisive one. Who was it who led United through those character-testing matches against Manchester City, Leeds and Oldham recently; games to judge the spirit and mental toughness of any mortal? Mark Hughes of course, living up to his nickname, Sparky, and perhaps forever establishing his reputation as a Manchester United legend.'

David Meek of the *Manchester Evening News*

'It is always satisfying to say I told you so – and that's precisely my feeling as I look at the marvellous form of Mark Hughes this season. I told Mark a year ago that I believed he was heading for probably the best season of his career because for the first time he had the right kind of partner up front. For too many seasons he laboured as either the lone-ranger up front or alongside players who were strikers rather than creators. All this changed with the arrival of Eric Cantona who, in addition to being a remarkable goalscorer himself, plays like an old-fashioned inside-forward – creating, passing and generally prompting with a vision and switch of play second to none. Mark Hughes has jumped at the opportunity and has himself become much more of a complete player making and taking goals as well as leading the line with refined skill and strength.'

My Career Record

Manchester United

Season	League		League Cup		FA Cup		Europe		Total	
	Apps	Gls	Apps	Gls	Apps	Gls	Apps	Gls	Apps	Gls
1983/84	7(4)	4	1(1)	1	0	0	2(2)	0	10(7)	5
1984/85	38	16	2	3	7	4	8	2	55	25
1985/86	40	17	2	0	3	1	0	0	45	18
1986/87 } 1987/88	Barcelona & Bayern Munich									
1988/89	38	14	3	0	7	2	0	0	48	16
1989/90	36(1)	13	3	0	8	2	0	0	47(1)	15
1990/91	29(2)	10	9	6	3	2	7(1)	3	48(3)	21
1991/92	38(1)	11	6	0	2(1)	1	4	2	50(2)	14
1992/93	41	15	3	1	2	0	2	0	48	16
1993/94	36	12	8	5	6	3	2	0	52	20
Total	303(8)	112	37(1)	16	38(1)	15	25(3)	7	403(13)	150

LEAGUE DÉBUT (as substitute)
Saturday 21 January 1984 v. SOUTHAMPTON (Old Trafford). Won 3-2
UNITED: Bailey, Duxbury, Moses, Wilkins, Moran, Hogg, Robson,
Muhren, Stapleton, Whiteside, Graham.
Substitute: Hughes (for Whiteside).   Scorers: Robson, Muhren, Stapleton.
SOUTHAMPTON: Shilton, Mills, Dennis, Agboola, Armstrong K.,
Wright, Holmes, Moran, Worthington, Armstrong D., Wallace.
Substitute: Puckett (for Armstrong K.).   Scorer: Moran 2.

LEAGUE DÉBUT (in starting line-up)
Saturday 10 March 1984 v. LEICESTER CITY (Old Trafford). Won 2-0
UNITED: Bailey, Duxbury, Albiston, Wilkins, Moran, Hogg, Robson,
Muhren, Stapleton, Hughes, Moses.
Substitute: Graham (not used).   Scorers: Moses, Hughes.
LEICESTER CITY: Wallington, Smith R., Wilson, MacDonald, Hazell,
O'Neill, Lynex, Lineker, Smith A., Feeley, Peake.
Substitute: English (for Feeley).

Wales

	Apps	Gls
1983/84	2	2
1984/85	7	3
1985/86	3	1
1986/87	2	0
1987/88	6	2
1988/89	5	0
1989/90	3	0
1990/91	7	1
1991/92	8	0
1992/93	7	3
1993/94	3	0
Total	53	12

HUGHESIE

FULL INTERNATIONAL DÉBUT
Saturday 2 May 1984 HOME INTERNATIONAL CHAMPIONSHIP
v. ENGLAND (The Racecourse Ground, Wrexham). Won 1–0
WALES: Southall (Everton), Phillips (Plymouth Argyle), Jones (Chelsea),
James (Stoke City), Hopkins (Fulham), Ratcliffe (Everton),
Davies G. (Fulham), Davies A. (Manchester United), Rush (Liverpool),
Thomas (Chelsea), Hughes (Manchester United).
Scorer: Hughes.
ENGLAND: Shilton (Southampton), Duxbury (Manchester United),
Kennedy (Liverpool), Lee (Liverpool), Martin (West Ham United),
Wright (Southampton), Wilkins (Manchester United),
Gregory (Queens Park Rangers), Walsh (Luton Town), Woodcock (Arsenal),
Armstrong D. (Southampton).
Substitutes: Fenwick (Queens Park Rangers) for Martin,
Blissett (Watford) for Armstrong D.